A Multiple-Continuous Offense
For High School Basketball

A Multiple-Continuous Offense
For High School Basketball

JAMES CATHCART

Parker Publishing Company, Inc.   WEST NYACK, N.Y.

PRINTED IN THE UNITED STATES OF AMERICA

BC

Guide to a
Winning Offense

No one offensive attack exists that will automatically produce a winning team. There are so many variables involved in the game of basketball that a coach cannot expect to find a "magic" combination of plays that will instantly enable his team to win all of its games. However, most coaches are always looking for something a little different from the ordinary offensive patterns and are willing to try a variety of combinations that might *help* them have a successful season.

This book will describe an offensive attack that has proved successful from my standpoint as a coach. It differs from a simple pattern in that it was developed around the concepts of (1) having one basic offensive attack that would be comprehensive enough to serve all major purposes of a good offense, and (2) eliminating the need of having to use additional plays or patterns to counteract such threats as oversized players, varying defensive tactics, etc. The Multiple-Continuous Offense has accomplished these objectives for my teams even better than I had hoped when I first put it together.

The numerous inquiries received from other coaches about this offense have encouraged me to write this book. I felt that their interest was indicative of the overall appeal of the Multiple-Continuous Offense, and that a comprehensive book about it would be beneficial to any coach who is looking for a multi-purpose offensive system that is somewhat different from the basic offenses that are in general usage in high school basketball today.

You will find that the advantages of using this offense are

many and varied. First of all, a requisite of any good offensive attack is that it must provide sound, balanced shooting opportunities from several areas of the court. The M-C Offense definitely meets this requirement; it gives each of the five men from two to six different shots from various floor positions throughout the pattern. Other assets of the offense that are enlarged upon in this book include pattern balance and continuity, the many options, the element of surprise inherent in the offense, and the consistency of the pattern movement of each player. Additional features that will be of interest to all coaches are (1) the fact that the offense is harder than usual for opponents to scout; (2) it is designed for the average player (size- and ability-wise), not for any one "hot" shooter or extra-tall inside man; and (3) by using selected options, the coach will be able to combat all types of defense effectively.

The purpose of this book is to serve as an all-encompassing guide to the use of the Multiple-Continuous Offense. As you read it you will find:

1. Detailed descriptions of the options and the techniques to be used in running them.
2. Instructions on how to set up the offense and tips on selecting personnel, teaching the pattern, and "selling" the offense to the players.
3. Drills specifically tailored to the pattern.
4. Information on which options will be best to use against each of the common defensive setups.
5. Coaching strategy that will make the offensive pattern run smoothly and be utilized to full potential.

In short, this book will give the coach all the tools he will need to build an effective and efficient attack using the Multiple-Continuous Offense. When properly executed, this pattern will help his team win.

Jim Cathcart

Contents

11

A Multiple-Continuous Offense
For High School Basketball

1

Analyzing the Advantages of the Multiple-Continuous Offense

Are you, as a basketball coach, tired of changing your offensive attack each time you encounter a different type of defense? Would you like to find a pattern that you can teach your players at the beginning of the season and use all year long without having to add new maneuvers as the season progresses? Is your personnel less than ideal? Do you lack the size you would prefer to have? Or do you have a good personnel potential and want to try something a little different from your regular offensive attack? Are you looking for an offense that is harder than usual to scout? Do you like to run a fast-moving, patterned offense?

If your answer to any of these questions is "yes," then you may find what you are looking for in the Multiple-Continuous Offense.

What is the multiple-continuous offense?

The name "Multiple-Continuous" is used to describe this offense—the "multiple" pointing out the many options included in the pattern and the "continuous" indicating the continuity that is present in the shift from one option to another. You might say that it is a multiple offense with continuing options from each phase of attack. It consists of several basic maneuvers with which to begin the attack, plus a succession of specific "follow-up" options to be used with each initial option. When executed properly, it will produce a smooth, fast-moving offensive attack with numerous scoring opportunities that will be harder than usual for the opponent to defense.

How it compares to a basic 1-3-1 offense

Because the Multiple-Continuous Offense was developed from the basic 1-3-1 offensive pattern that is so prevalent in both high school and college basketball today, many coaches, when scouting it, will call it a typical 1-3-1. The Multiple-Continuous pattern, however, is not run from the regular 1-3-1 setup. Figure 1 * shows the basic 1-3-1 formation with the outside man out front, the low post inside, and the two wing men lined up on each side of the high post man along the free-throw line extended.

The Multiple-Continuous setup is illustrated in Figure 2. Although the positions of the two post men and one of the wing men are nearly the same as in the 1-3-1, the outside man has been pulled over to the right, and the wing man on the right-hand side of the court has been moved back toward midcourt so that he can function as a guard. Since these two men have been offset, much of the balance of the basic 1-3-1 is gone; the Multiple-Continuous setup leans toward an overload situation.

With the offset, the personnel now consists of the two outside men (1 and 2), the wing man (3), the high post man (4), and the low post man (5). All five players will always assume the positions on offense shown in Figure 2 to begin the pattern (except when there is an opportunity for a fast break) because

---

* Illustrations are identified according to chapter by the first of the two numbers in each caption. *Figure 5-2*, for example, refers to the second illustration in Chapter 5.

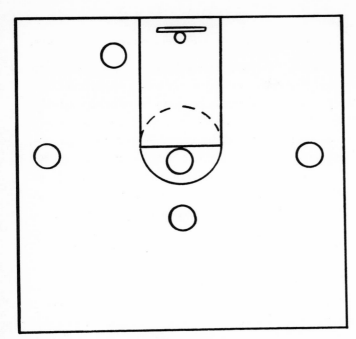

Figure 1-1
Basic 1-3-1 Offensive Setup

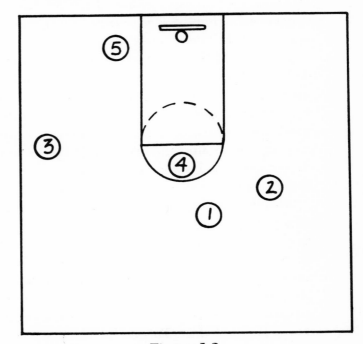

Figure 1-2
Basic Setup of Multiple-Continuous Offense

each initial option of the pattern is designed to be run from this formation. The options are arranged so as to take full advantage of the overload, and more emphasis is placed on inside movement than is usual in a basic 1-3-1 pattern.

Because of the positions taken by the high post and low post men in the basic setup, this offense can also be confused with a tandem post offense. Although the pattern may reflect its influence at times, it definitely cannot be labeled as such. Neither is there a consistent interchange between the post men nor is the pattern completely dependent upon the moves and screens of these two players, as is the case with the tandem post.

Is this offense similar to a shuffle?

Some coaches, after seeing the Multiple-Continuous pattern in action, have even tried to refer to it as a form of the shuffle offense that was introduced several years ago and which is now being used by many coaches as their basic offense. Actually, the two patterns are entirely different, both in pattern movement and in the spot shooting of players from the pattern. In the shuffle, one player makes his initial move and then assumes the responsibility of another player. In other words, 1 becomes 3, and 3 becomes 5 (depending on the move and on how the coach numbers his players). This player identity-responsibility switch does not occur in the Multiple-Continuous attack. For example, 1 does not take on the responsibility of another player after the first pass or the second pass is made; he continues to his area and remains 1. Also, this offense has more continuity than a shuffle, and the key players on each option act as either screener or shooter in their basic offensive moves.

The reason why many coaches will try to connect this offense with the shuffle probably lies in their interpretation of the first move made on one of the initial options as a *"Shuffle Cut."* Actually, it will be a *"Give and Go"* move (see Figure 3): 1 passes to 2, moves over the screen set by the high post man, and heads for the basket. This option has possibly caused the con-

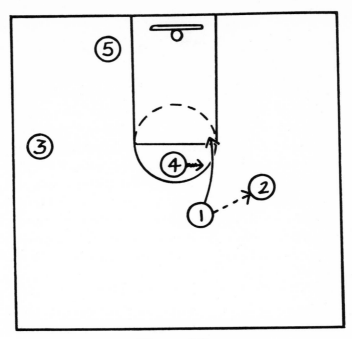

Figure 1-3
Give and Go Option Often Confused
with Shuffle Cut

fusion, but when you re-examine Figure 2, it is obvious that the shuffle offense could not be run from this setup. Therefore, you can see that there is absolutely no similarity between the Multiple-Continuous and the shuffle offenses.

How this offense can frustrate your opponent

The primary advantage of the Multiple-Continuous Offense lies in its ability to keep the defense guessing and wondering what the next move will be. Because it embodies a variety of options, the offensive players are often able to surprise the opponent as well as keep him confused. Many high school teams (and some college teams as well) employ only one or two phases of attack in their pattern work. In that case, if a play or its option fails to work out, the players will either free-lance for a basket or they will be forced to bring the ball out to the starting point of their pattern and begin again. This situation will not be so common when using the Multiple-Continuous Offense.

19

To begin with, you may start your attack with any one of the initial options. If the first option is unsuccessful, you will have from one to four follow-up options (depending on which phase you are running) to try before having to begin the pattern again. Even then you can select another initial option if the situation warrants it; you need not run the same series of options over and over again. Your players will be in position to move immediately into the subsequent option or options, and they will know exactly what moves to make because these successive options are an integral part of the pattern. Therein lies the continuity of the offense as well as the element of surprise. Your opponent may adjust to one option or series of options only to find that you have switched to a different phase of attack. Or, if they have caught on to your moves, you can turn the pattern over completely—that will definitely keep the defense honest. You will keep your opponent constantly wondering which way you will go and what you will do with the ball when you get there. You will find that you will be able to take advantage of overplaying defenses; you can pick up easy baskets if you catch the defense playing the play.

The very fact that you can keep your opponent off balance and confused is what makes the offense so hard to scout. A future opponent can watch you play and diagram every move you make on a given night, but he has no way of knowing which options you will concentrate on or how you will mix them up when he plays you. The element of surprise, the continuity, and the many options will give you a great advantage over your opponent.

Other advantages of the multiple-continuous offense

Designed for Average Personnel

Every coach is always looking for the offensive pattern that best fits his personnel. Obviously, a coach with ideal material has no problem in this area, but most high school teams and many college teams simply do not have an ideal situation in terms of the size and ability of the players. Therefore, the coach faces the universal problem of trying to settle on an offense that will best suit the players he has as well as one that will help him win ball games. The trial-and-error method is used by many coaches in the continual search for a winning combination of players and for an offense that fits their abilities. They will go through an entire season attempting to find the answer by shuffling their players and trying many types of patterns.

If your personnel is less than ideal, the Multiple-Continuous Offense could solve your problems (or at least some of your problems) because it can be very effective even when the players' qualifications (size- and ability-wise) are only average or a little above. Your low post man need not be a giant nor do the outside men have to be dead-eye shooters. Good attitude, quickness, and team cooperation are the most important qualities necessary to make this offensive attack successful. On the other hand, if your players have these qualities plus unusual height and/or exceptionally fine shooting ability, you will have an extra advantage over your opponents with this offense.

Provides Good Rebounding Positioning

All coaches are concerned with the rebounding strength on offense as well as on defense. With this offense, rebounding positions for each player are set for every option. Three men will always be on the inside in good rebounding position, regardless of the option that is used. Some coaches will have four offensive players crash the boards, but since the back court is always vulnerable to the fast break, this pattern has two men back at all times in the fast-break defensive balance positions to provide sound floor balance. This will tend to discourage your opponent from using his fast break every time you put the ball on the boards.

Reduces the Threat of the Defense's Big Man

Most defensive teams will put their big man on the offensive low post man so that he will be able to stay in close to rebound and can check the layups of the outside offensive guards. The Multiple-Continuous attack can minimize the effectiveness of this big defensive man to some extent because on most options the offensive low post man (5) will pull out toward the corner, forcing the big man to move with him. This will give your guards room to maneuver for their options and will give the offensive players a better chance to rebound their missed baskets.

Effective Against All Types of Defense

Another advantage of the Multiple-Continuous Offense is that it is effective against the various types of zone defenses as well as the many variations of the man-to-man defense that confront the coach. The pressure defense, tight man-to-man, switching man-to-man, and the different types of trapping defenses are an ever-present problem to any coach. Often he feels that his offense must be changed from game to game in order to cope with these many defenses. As a result, he will find himself trying so many offensive combinations that he may discover that he has moved completely away from his basic attack. This can consume much valuable coaching time and can have an adverse effect on team morale. With the Multiple-Continuous Offense you will not have this problem; you can spend your practice time perfecting this one offensive pattern. By using the options specified in Chapters 6 and 7 against the respective defenses, you will find that you will be able to effectively combat any defensive setup you come up against.

2

Organizing the Multiple-
Continuous Offense

As you become familiar with
the options of the Multiple-Continuous pattern, you will un-
derstand why much of the success of your attack will depend
on an efficient organization of your players, with each man
playing the position that best suits his talents and abilities.
Since the Multiple-Continuous Offense is a *complete* offensive
attack, it is most important that it be set up in the very best way
possible at the beginning of the pre-season workouts so that you
can concentrate on perfecting the options without having to
waste time shuffling your players around.

The purpose of this chapter is to help you select the right
player for each position of this offense and to give you a comprehensive picture of the general responsibilities and playing
area of each man. Tips on teaching the pattern and on making
necessary adjustments will also be covered. The position analysis will be especially helpful when you introduce the offense to
the players, because it will show them exactly what part they
each will play in making the offense work and the need for
every man to put forth his best effort in order to win.

An analysis of each position

To begin with, you can get a clearer picture of each man's role in the pattern by analyzing the positions individually. A thorough knowledge of the shooting areas and the responsibilities to the pattern of each position will be invaluable when the time comes for you to select the best players to fill these spots. As the moves and assignments of each player on every option are covered in detail in "The Outside Attack" and "The Inside Attack," there is no need for a repetition here. What concerns you at this point is a rundown on the contribution of each position to the pattern as a whole.

Consistency of Pattern Movement

In Figures 1 through 5, all the different moves each player will make throughout the pattern have been combined into one diagram. Only the actual movement of the player's body from one point to another which is specifically called for by the options is included. The shaded area around these moves outlines his general playing area; this allows for adjustments or exaggerations of the original pattern move. You can see how the pattern movement of each man takes place in a precise section of the playing court. There is an exception in the case of the 2 man; he will clear to the opposite side on two options. Otherwise, his moves are also confined to a definite area.

The fact that each man has a particular area in which to make his moves will facilitate teaching the offense to your players. A player's moves may be varied, but they will more or less consistently follow a pattern within his own playing zone. He will not be in a different section of the court from option to option. Also, when a comparison of the five diagrams is made, it is obvious that even though each man works in his own area (with the inevitable overlapping around the basket area), the entire forecourt is utilized by the offensive pattern.

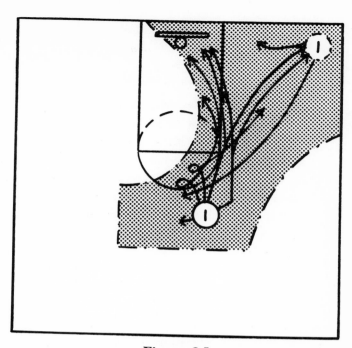

Figure 2-1
Pattern Moves and Playing Area—Player 1

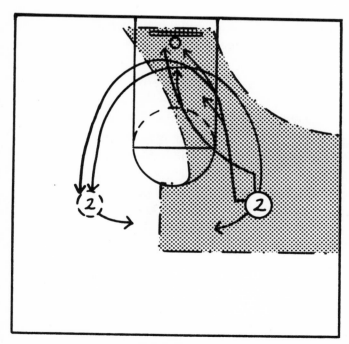

Figure 2-2
Pattern Moves and Playing Area—Player 2

Responsibility of Each Position to the Pattern

The following position breakdown will give you a better idea of how important each position is to the team as a whole. This will be of great help to you when you introduce the offense to the players because you will be able to stress the role each one plays in making the pattern work; every player will feel that he is a real part of the team. This factor should contribute much to the overall attitude of the team, for players who work together and depend on each other rather than on one or two to "do it all" will inevitably develop confidence and will take pride in putting forth a team effort to win games.

Note: The following breakdown includes the general responsibilities and shooting opportunities for each man on the *basic* options. When adjustments are made against specific defensive attacks, the shooting opportunities, in particular, may vary some.

PLAYER 1 (Outside Man)

Always begins the pattern when the ball is brought down the court; he either originates the outside options or passes to 3 for the Inside Attack.

Has a greater variety of moves and responsibilities than the other players.

Has two main playing positions—out front and in the corner.

Is designated as shooter on two options; he can be the shooter on three other options where there are alternatives. (He ordinarily shoots on the outside options only.)

Will drop back to help set up back-court balance on most options as soon as the ball is put on the boards.

PLAYER 2 (Outside Man)

Has two primary tasks—outside coverage and passing maneuvers with 1. He will cover the outside from his regular position except when he clears to the other side.

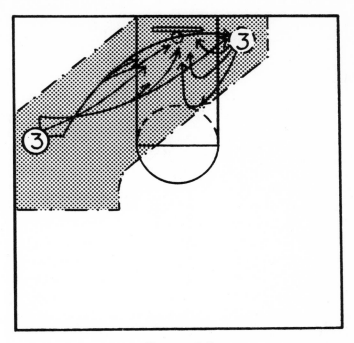

Figure 2-3
Pattern Moves and Playing Area—Player 3

Has few specific moves; his job is to remain in his position for balance and passing; he has no rebounding responsibility.

Will be the shooter on two options—the only times he will make a move toward the basket area (except to clear).

PLAYER 3 (Wing Man)

Has responsibilities on both the inside and the outside options in terms of moves off the pattern; he probably moves more on the Inside Attack.

Has two main playing spots—his wing position and the opposite low post; all his moves are in a zone between those two positions.

Is responsible for getting the ball to 5 on all inside options.

Will move from wing to opposite low post on each option of the Inside Attack, screening for 5 as he goes.

Is designated as the shooter on four options; he can be the shooter on three others.

27

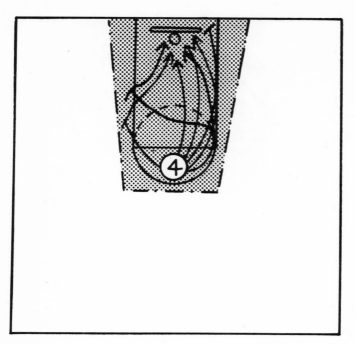

Figure 2-4
Pattern Moves and Playing Area—Player 4

Figure 2-5
Pattern Moves and Playing Area—Player 5

Will have rebounding assignments on at least five options, depending on whether he shoots or passes off.

PLAYER 4 (High Post Man)

Makes all of his moves from high post towards the baseline in the lane area.

Mainly functions as a screener and a rebounder. He will screen for 1 on three options, for 3 on two options, and for 2 on one option. As he moves towards the goal on the inside options, he will often screen for 5 when 5 pulls way out and up toward the free-throw line extended.

Will be the shooter on one option and can be the shooter on one other; he plays the role of rebounder on the rest of the options.

PLAYER 5 (Low Post Man)

Has few moves on most of the outside options; he stays at low post for the rebound. He shoots on one option and can be the shooter on one other option.

Is the playmaker for the Inside Attack; he will always receive the ball from 3 and either shoot or pass off.

Will be the shooter in three of the five inside options, although he does have the alternative of passing off to another player each time if he is unable to get the shot off.

Will be responsible for rebounding whenever he is not the shooter (if he can get to the boards when he shoots, so much the better).

Will sometimes pull way up toward midcourt with the ball, temporarily exchange positions with 4, and remain there to shoot or while an outside option (for instance) is run.

Qualities to look for in your players

The next step in organizing the offense will be to make an evaluation of the skills and abilities of your players so that you can determine which players can play each of the positions to best advantage. First of all, consider the three general areas on which most coaches rely when choosing their players: attitude, physical attributes, and ball-handling skills. Here is how they relate to the M-C pattern.

Attitude

The most important factor in making any offense successful is good player attitude. This is especially true in the case of the Multiple-Continuous Offense because its effectiveness depends in a large part on a "team" effort. The presence of one or two players who think they must shoot the ball every time they get their hands on it, regardless, can wreck an otherwise smoothly operating pattern and can defeat the purpose of having a pattern at all. You will want players on your team who love the game enough to buckle down to the disciplines of the pattern and who are unselfish enough to have confidence in the moves and abilities of their teammates as well as their own. Because this pattern involves so many options, it is most important that each time the players are on offense they move the ball to the man who will have the *best* shot (not just any shot) off the pattern under the circumstances prevalent at that particular time. In order to accomplish this, each player must be willing to "give" a little and do what is best for the team as a whole. When selecting players to run the M-C Offense, look for boys who want to play for the sake of the team, not for the sake of themselves.

Physical Attributes

The height and overall size of your team is important, but not so important as attitude and enthusiasm. Height need not be your main concern because this offense was designed to be used with the average-sized boys (5'8" to 6' outside men and 6'1" to 6'2" or over post men) who are available to the majority of coaches. It is true that you will want some height on the inside for rebounding and defensive purposes—every coach does.

Therefore, when you are attempting to make a choice between players where all other considerations are equal, you naturally would select the taller and stronger player. If you do have an exceptionally tall post man, you can utilize his size by concentrating on the inside options; in all other cases you can use the pattern with confidence with average-sized personnel.

Ball-Handling Skills

Again, this pattern was designed to make a team of average or a little above average ball handlers more effective. If you have an outstanding shooter, you can put him in one of the guard positions or in the wing position and concentrate on the options where he is the shooter. Otherwise you should select your players in this area for their ball-handling and shooting capability in general. Quickness in movement with and without the ball is very important to the pattern, and a quick-thinking player with leadership potential will be a tremendous asset in running the options.

Fit the player to the position

The following lists summarize the minimum physical qualities and ball-playing techniques that a player should have in order to play the respective position effectively.

The Outside Guards (1 and 2)

Handles the ball with confidence
Is an average outside shooter
Can shoot jumpers on the move
Uses both hands effectively in ball handling
Has better than average quickness
Is able to use the reverse with the ball to get the quick jumper
    (1 only)
Can start the offensive pattern either to the right or to the left
    (1 only)

The Wing Man (3)

Is an average outside shooter
Handles the ball with confidence
Uses both hands effectively in ball handling
Passes the ball effectively
Has a good knowledge of setting screens
Is an average rebounder

The High Post Man (4)

Is a better than average rebounder
Knows how to set strong screens and has the ability to get good
  position after screening
Is an average ball handler
Is an average shooter in the basket area (from six feet out to
  the baseline)
Has good quickness
Is stronger physically than the other players

The Low Post Man (5)

Is a better than average ball handler
Is stronger on the boards than any other player
Is able to go both ways with the ball
Has the ability to shoot jumpers from ten feet out to the base-
  line effectively
Possesses good overall quickness
Has good jumping ability
Has the ability to quickly pick out the open man on offense

Other Considerations

In addition, you might keep in mind the fact that the 1 man
and the 5 man (with the wing man running a close third) tend
to hold the dominant roles throughout the pattern, even though
a good performance is necessary from all five players. If you
have two guards for the outside positions who shoot equally
well, put the boy who has the most self-confidence and who

possesses more leadership of the two in the 1 spot. The 2 position, although definitely important to the offense, does not require quite as much level-headedness and quick thinking as does the 1 position. Also, you will want to put your most versatile big boy in the low post position (5), for it is he who makes the split-second decisions on the inside options. He will probably shoot the ball more than any other player and should also be your best rebounder.

Tips on teaching the offense to the players

Introducing the Offense

All coaches have different ways of introducing a new offensive attack to their players. Whether you are accustomed to using demonstrations, chalk talks, film, printed materials, or a combination of all of these methods makes little difference. You can use the method that you feel is most effective. However, here are some suggestions that will be of help in "selling" the M-C Offense to the team:

1. Let the players know that you are sold on the Multiple-Continuous Offense and are convinced that it can help them win.

2. Impress on them that it is a "team" offense designed for all five players, not for one or two in particular. Tell them that each player will have an important contribution to make to the team as a whole and that they must all work together to produce the best results.

3. Show each player the position on the floor from which he will make his moves. Draw a diagram similar to Figures 1-5 to give them an idea of each man's playing area.

4. Go over the responsibilities of each position with emphasis on the fact that each man will have several opportunities to be the shooter. Also let them know that each player has definite responsibilities on each option.

5. Stress the importance a good attitude plays and how the team must always get the ball to the man who has the best chance of scoring.

Teaching the Pattern

After you have familiarized the players with the offense as suggested above, they will be ready to learn the moves of each option. The specialized drills presented in "Offensive Drills and Techniques" are an excellent way in which to begin teaching the pattern options. When the players have mastered these nine drills, they will have learned four major options, and the remainder of the options should come easy for them. The most effective way to teach the other options is to have the players run each option over and over, until they have the moves perfected and each move becomes automatic. Then you can combine the options which complement each other and run them as a unit. As soon as the players have a thorough knowledge of the moves and techniques of every option and how each option fits into the pattern, you will be ready to put the pattern together and begin your intensive pattern work and half-court scrimmages.

Adjustments

As you teach the options, you should make the players aware of adjustments they may need to make in order to counteract the various defensive tactics they will meet. For example, if a team is playing you tight and cuts off an essential pass, your players must be flexible enough to make a temporary adjustment that will allow the pattern to run as it should. The following situations illustrate three common instances where adjustments will be necessary.

Situation 1

PROBLEM: The offense is attempting to run the give and go options of the Outside Attack. X-2 is overplaying 2, cutting

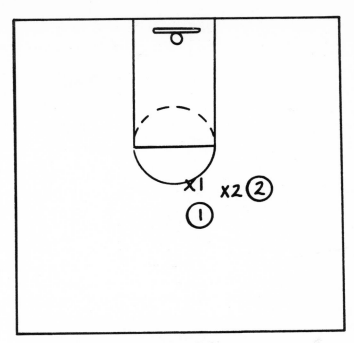

Figure 2-6a
Situation 1—Problem

Figure 2-6b
Situation 1—Adjustment

off 1's pass to 2 and keeping the option from being started (Figure 6a).

ADJUSTMENT: The 2 man clears, taking his defensive man with him. This leaves 1 room in which to maneuver (Figure 6b). 1 now has a one-on-one with X-1 and can use the reverse over 4's screen for a jumper or a layup.

Situation 2

PROBLEM: X-5 is overplaying the low post man (5) and is discouraging the pass from 3 which is essential in order to use the Inside Attack (Figure 7a).

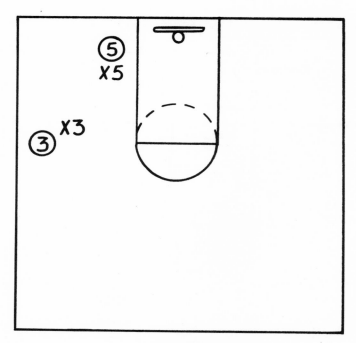

Figure 2-7a
Situation 2—Problem

ADJUSTMENT: 5 will pull out along the baseline to receive the pass from 3. A two-on-two situation now exists with the wing man and the low post man. 3 passes to 5 as usual, then screens and goes through (Figure 7b). 5 will be able to run the inside options from this extended position as well as he does from his regular position.

Situation 3

PROBLEM: X-3 is overplaying 3; 3 is unable to receive the pass from 1 that begins the Inside Attack (Figure 8a).

ADJUSTMENT: 3 clears and goes through to his opposite low post position. 1, who has the ball, moves to the wing position

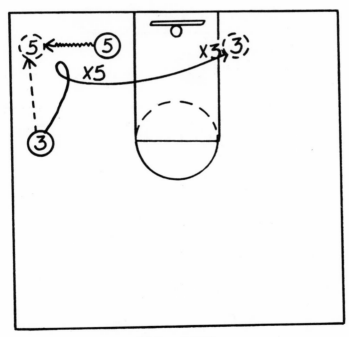

Figure 2-7b
Situation 2—Adjustment

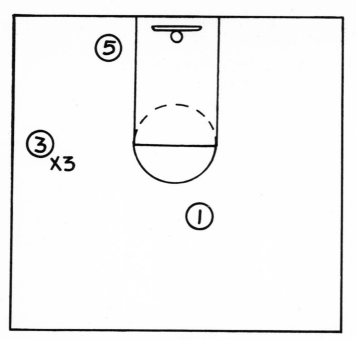

Figure 2-8a
Situation 3—Problem

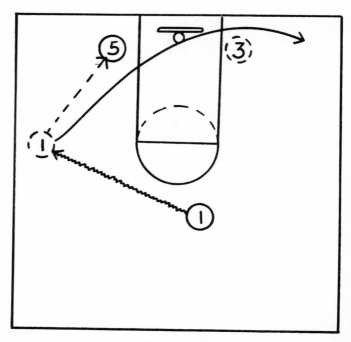

Figure 2-8b
Situation 3—Adjustment

and makes the pass to the low post man (Figure 8b). Now the inside options can be run just as if 3 had made the pass to 5. After 1 passes the ball, he goes through to the corner —his regular position for the inside options.

3

Offensive Drills and Techniques for the M-C Offense

Drills are a very important part of the daily practice session. Every coach uses a variety of basic drills that stress conditioning, agility and quickness, shooting, rebounding, defensive moves, and other ball-handling techniques. Too often, however, with so many drills to choose from, the coach has difficulty in limiting his selection of offensive drills to those which will most benefit his program as a whole. Also, many coaches tend to think of drills merely as routines that develop fundamental skills and overlook the possibility of using them as "pattern-teaching" devices. There is no argument with the fact that some basic drills are a necessary part of every practice, but the coach who plans to use a comprehensive pattern for his offensive attack should also use some specialized drills that are correlated with or built around his pattern moves.

This chapter will include both types of drills: specialized or pattern-oriented drills geared to the Multiple-Continuous

41

Offense (on which most emphasis is placed) and selected basic drills which can be used as necessary for work on general techniques.

Specialized drills

The Purpose of Pattern-oriented Drills

The concept of using pattern-oriented drills may be new to many coaches, but a short explanation will quickly reveal their importance. These are drills which concentrate on distinct moves and techniques which will be utilized in the pattern exactly as they are run in the drills. Several of the drills will consist of a specific option run in drill formation; others are basic drills which have been adapted and expanded to fit certain phases of the Multiple-Continuous attack. Each drill has a direct carryover to the pattern itself. Besides giving instructions on methods of execution, the explanations of the drills also contain explicit directions on how the moves should be made and the techniques that should be stressed. All of these drills are designed to familiarize the players with the different phases of the pattern as well as to develop the skills they will need to have in order to run it effectively.

Advantages of Using These Drills

The use of these pattern-oriented drills can improve your practice sessions in four ways:

SIMPLIFIES TEACHING THE PATTERN

Perhaps most important from the coach's viewpoint is the fact that these drills can give you a head start on your pattern work at the beginning of the season. When you are ready to teach the pattern itself, the players will recognize many of the moves as ones they have learned in the drills and have already perfected.

STIMULATES PLAYER INTEREST

Putting the pattern moves into drill form breaks the monotony of the constant repetition of common everyday drills. Even as the season progresses, the players will have a feeling of accomplishment as they run the pattern-oriented drills because they will be working on moves that they know will help them run the offensive pattern to best advantage.

FAMILIARIZES PLAYERS WITH MOVES OF ALL POSITIONS

As the players work on these drills, they will be learning and making the moves of the other positions as well as those of the specific position they have been designated to play. This helps give them a clearer picture of all facets of the pattern and will improve their spontaneity and continuity in running the options.

SAVES PRACTICE TIME

By concentrating on these specific drills, you can give your players their drill work and some pattern work all at once. You can then devote more of your valuable practice time to other phases of the game.

Nine specialized drills geared to the multiple-continuous pattern

Note: In the diagrams and explanations of the drills, the offensive players will be numbered to correspond with the position they occupy in the basic pattern setup. (left guard—1, right guard—2, wing man—3, high post—4, and low post—5)

Outside reverse drills

Here are three drills that use the outside reverse (which will be made by the 1 man in the pattern). Maneuvering for and making the quick jumper or the layup are the primary objectives of these drills. Also, they will show the offensive players the reverse, with stress on whipping the defensive man. They can be used both with and without the defense; have the players run each phase of the drill dummy five times and then repeat, using the defense. You can make the drills competitive by giving the offense two points when they score and the defense two points for failure of the offense to score. At the end of the drill, the coach announces the total points. This provides an incentive for the players to work hard both on offense and on defense.

Specialized Drill 1: Outside Reverse with Layup

A. Without defense (Figure 1)

1. Have the players form two lines. Line A (the outside men) will form behind the 1 man position, and Line B (the inside men) forms in the left back side of the court, with the first man in Line B moving up to play the high post position.

2. Using the left hand dribble, 0-1 drives with the ball to the left of 0-4. Then, using the reverse dribble with the right hand, he comes back over the top of 0-4 and around him and drives to the basket for a layup.

3. After the first two men have completed their maneuvers, they go to the end of their respective lines, and the drill continues with the next man up in each line.

B. With defense (Figure 2)

1. The setup is the same as in Drill 1-A except that in Line A the first player will be on defense and the second player on offense.

2. 0-1's moves are the same as in Drill 1-A. 0-4 screens X-1 and tries to hang him up exactly as he would in a game situation.

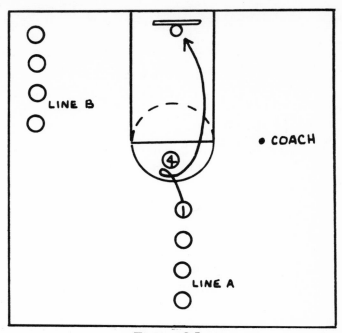

Figure 3-1
Specialized Drill 1-A
Outside Reverse with Layup
(without defense)

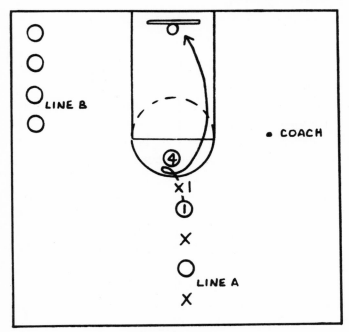

Figure 3-2
Specialized Drill 1-B
Outside Reverse with Layup
(with defense)

3. After 0-1 has gone for the layup, both he and X-1 go to the end of Line A, and 0-4 goes to the end of Line B as before. After the first time around, the players will switch on offense and defense so that each man in Line A will have a chance to run both phases of the drill.

Specialized Drill 2: Outside Reverse with Jumper

A. Without defense (Figure 3)

The procedure for this drill is the same as that for Drill 1-A except that 0-1 pulls up for a quick jumper at the top of the key after the reverse instead of going in for the layup.

B. With defense (Figure 4)

The drill is just like Drill 1-B except for the substitution of a quick jumper for the layup.

Specialized Drill 3: Outside Reverse with Jumper or Layup (Combination Drill) (no diagram)

Drill 3 is a combination of Drills 1-B and 2-B. The mechanics are the same, but 0-1 will take *either* the jumper or the layup, depending on the hand signal given by the coach as he starts his reverse. An open hand is the signal for 0-1 to work for the layup, and a closed fist indicates that he is to work for the jumper. The hand signals are used so that X-1 will not know in advance which shot 0-1 will attempt. Since the drill is to be run at full speed, it takes on the appearance of a true game situation, and the players are always quick to pick up the carryover to the pattern option. They will be eager to show their competitiveness in this drill. Most offensive phases are covered here (cutting, screening, faking, and shooting), and the defensive phase will be of equal value to the team.

After your players have Drills 1 and 2 down pat and are

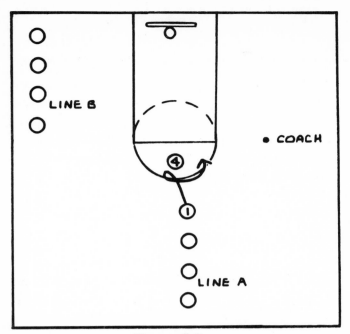

Figure 3-3
Specialized Drill 2-A
Outside Reverse with Jumper
(without defense)

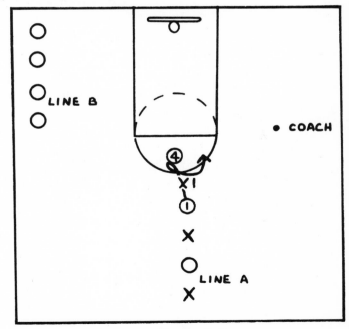

Figure 3-4
Specialized Drill 2-B
Outside Reverse with Jumper
(with defense)

thoroughly acquainted with the moves of the *Outside Reverse* option, you need not use the drills separately in practice sessions. By using the combination, you will achieve the same (or better) results and will be able to save valuable practice time. Some coaches will refer to this drill as a one-on-one. It is that, but at the same time it has been adapted so that when you use it you are actually running an option of the Multiple-Continuous pattern.

Outside give and go drills

Specialized Drill 4: Give and Go Variation

This is a drill that should be used every day in practice because it has a tremendous carryover to the actual game situation. It is designed primarily for the outside guards and the post man. It will accomplish three objectives:

1. It acquaints the outside men and the post man with the individual moves of each of the three positions such as head fakes, body fakes, and foot fakes.
2. It gives the guards who will work together in game situations ball-handling experience with each other and helps them develop confidence in this area.
3. It teaches the three players a very important pattern option.

At first, the drill should be run dummy, with the coach paying particular attention to the passing, faking, timing, and cutting. After a short period, the pace of the drill can be stepped up and the defense can be added. The techniques can then be observed by the coach with the players going full speed. The passing phase, in particular, should be emphasized. Have the players use the quick right-hand bounce pass as well as the quick overhead pass and the high right-hand-over-the-right-shoulder pass. This drill relates directly to the *Give and Go Variation* option.

PROCEDURE

A. Without defense (Figure 5)

    1. Divide your squad into three groups. Line A (the inside men) will form in the left back side of the court; these players will function as high post men. Line B is placed behind the left guard (1 man) position, and Line C forms behind the right guard (2 man) position.

    2. 0-1 passes to 0-2, drives straight ahead at 0-4, cuts to either the right or the left of 0-4 toward the basket, and receives the return pass from 0-2.

    3. When the three players have completed Step 2, 0-4 goes to the end of his line (Line A), 0-1 goes to the end of Line C, and 0-2 goes to the end of Line B. The drill will continue until each player in Lines B and C has functioned as 0-1 and 0-2.

B. With defense (Figure 6)

    1. The setup is the same as in Drill 4-A except that in Lines B and C the first player will be on defense and the second player on offense.

    2. The moves of 0-1 and 0-2 will be the same as in Drill 4-A. 0-4 acts as screener; in doing so, he is quick to pick up the execution of the drill. He learns the all-important factor of timing and the individual moves of the outside guards and also gains confidence in working with each of them.

    3. The drill is run until each man has performed in Line B once and in Line C once. Then the players switch so that each one will have an opportunity to play offense and defense in each line.

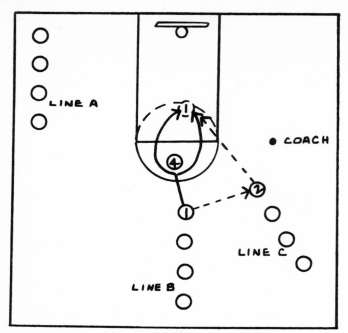

Figure 3-5
Specialized Drill 4-A
Give and Go Variation
(without defense)

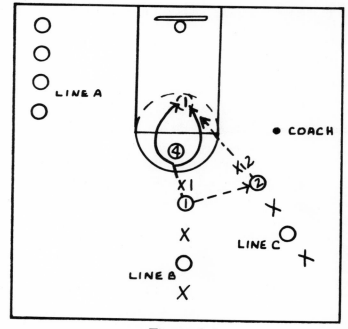

Figure 3-6
Specialized Drill 4-B
Give and Go Variation
(with defense)

Drills 5 and 6 are also designed for the outside guards and can be applied to either of the two *Give and Go* options. Their purpose is to teach the guards how to combat the tight man-to-man defense and the switching (overplaying) man-to-man defense which threaten to cut off the first pass of the outside options. The players are quick to pick up the carryover value of the drills to regular offensive pattern work. When half-court and full-court scrimmages begin, they see how important it is to know how to maneuver around the defense to complete that first pass.

Specialized Drill 5: Two-on-Two with Tight Man-to-Man Defense (Figure 7)

The reverse pivot and the screen are the key moves in Drill 5. Also important is 0-2's ability in timing to get free. X-1 is in a tight man-to-man and does not switch; this makes it difficult for him to cover both offensive guards. X-2 is screened out of the play. The success of this drill depends on the quickness of the offensive guards. Techniques to be stressed in the drill are (1) the reverse pivot and screen, (2) timing and faking, (3) quickness in movement, and (4) the hand-off pass.

PROCEDURE

1. Line up half of the players behind the left guard position and the others behind the right guard position. The first men in each line will play defense and the second men will play offense.
2. 0-1 drives with the ball to the inside leg of X-2, then reverse pivots to the inside, screening X-2. 0-2 body fakes X-2 to the baseline and comes over 0-1's screen. X-1 does not switch, thus 0-2 is open. 0-1 gives the ball to 0-2 on a hand-off. 0-2 is now free to shoot an outside jumper or go in for a layup.
3. The players will go to the end of the opposite line until each player has completed all phases of the drill.

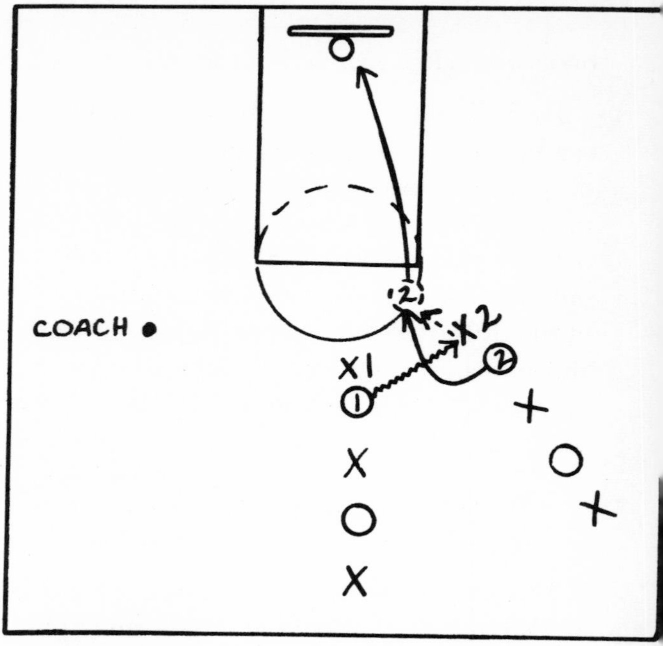

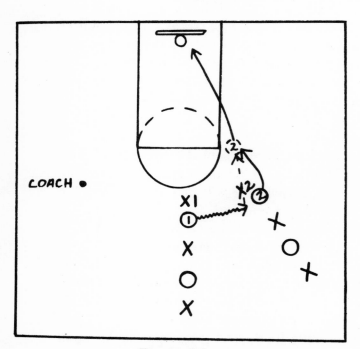

**Figure 3-7
Specialized Drill 5
Two-on-Two with Tight
Man-to-Man Defense**

**Figure 3-8
Specialized Drill 6
Two-on-Two with Switching
(Overplaying)
Man-to-Man Defense**

Specialized Drill 6: Two-on-Two with Switching
(Overplaying) Man-to-Man Defense (Figure 8)

Techniques to be stressed in Drill 6 include (1) quickness in observing positions of defensive men, (2) faking and timing, (3) execution of the quick overhead jump pass, and (4) general quickness of both offense and defense.

PROCEDURE

1. Setup is the same as in Drill 5.
2. 0-1 starts his drive with the ball toward 0-2 as if to set a screen. He observes the overplaying defensive position of X-2, who is waiting to switch. X-1 is still with 0-1, but is playing to pick up 0-2 off the screen. 0-2 immediately goes toward the basket around the outside of X-2. 0-1 pulls up with the ball and makes a quick jump pass to 0-2, who has faked as if to come off the screen but has headed to the basket. 0-2, after receiving the pass, continues to the basket for a layup or pulls up for a short jumper.
3. Player rotation is like that in Drill 5.

Wing man drill

Specialized Drill 7: Three Man Across
(A Three-on-Three Drill)

This drill is based on the *Three Man Across* option of the Outside Attack. Its purpose is to help the wing man develop the timing and the moves off the screen that will allow him to beat his defensive man and that will put him in position to receive the pass for his layup or jumper. The drill is also of value to the two post men. Effective screening, timing, and pattern moves are stressed over and over to the high post man. He learns that he must coordinate his move to screen with the wing man's move across the floor; his screen permits the wing man to run the option. The position of the low post man, while really not a part of the *Three Man Across* option, is included for the sake of the drill. His moves were added in order to make the drill more competitive and to stimulate greater interest on the part of the defense; this way the men on defense (in the drill) are unable to "play the play" every time the drill is run. At the same time, low post's participation in the drill gives him a chance to work on his individual moves. He will develop quickness, improve his timing on screens, and will have the opportunity to use the reverse move off a screen.

PROCEDURE

A. Without defense (Figure 9)

1. Divide the squad into two lines. Line A will be made up of the outside men and forms behind the wing (3 man) position. Line B (the post men) forms behind the low post (5 man) position. Before beginning the drill, one man moves up from Line A to be the passer, and a man moves up from Line B to play high post.

2. 0-4 rolls to the basket toward 0-3, hesitating to screen for him. 0-3 fakes toward the low post man, then comes off 0-4's screen and heads for the basket, watching for the pass for a quick jumper in the free-throw area or a layup. After 0-4 has screened for 0-3, he continues to the low post position and exchanges places with 0-5. 0-5 hesitates for 0-4's screen, watching 0-3's move. If 0-3 moves into the basket area without having received the ball, 0-5 moves quickly from the screen toward midcourt and receives the pass for a quick jumper in the free-throw area.

3. After the ball has been shot, the passer goes to the end of Line A, 0-3 becomes the passer, and 0-4 and 0-5 go to the end of Line B. The drill continues with the next men in each line.

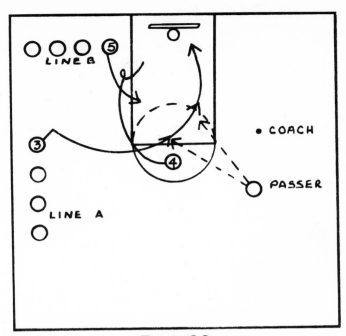

Figure 3-9
Specialized Drill 7-A
Three Man Across
(without defense)

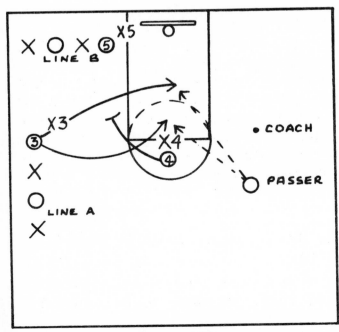

Figure 3-10
Specialized Drill 7-B
Three Man Across
(with defense)

B. With defense (Figure 10)

1. The alignment will be the same as in Drill 7-A
    except that seven men will be involved in the drill
    instead of four. Two men (0-3 and X-3) come up
    from Line A to the wing position, two men (0-4 and
    X-4) come up to the high post position from Line
    B, and two men (0-5 and X-5) remain at low post.
    Again a man from Line A is designated as passer
    the first time.

2. Some additional offensive moves will be necessary
    when the drill is run with the defense. 0-3 will move
    over the top of 0-4's screen unless X-3 is overplay-
    ing him. In that case, he cuts behind the screen.
    The type of shot taken by 0-3 will depend on when
    he receives the ball from the passer and on where
    he loses X-3 on the screen. 0-5 keys on 0-3's move.
    If 0-3 has beaten his man for the layup but does not
    receive the pass from the passer, then 0-5 either
    moves over the top of 0-4's screen, or he can hesi-
    tate and roll back on a reverse move (Figure 11).
    In both cases he will be looking for the ball from
    the passer for a jumper.

3. After these seven players have completed the drill,
    the passer and X-3 go to the end of Line A, 0-3
    becomes the passer, and the other four players go
    to the end of Line B. The players alternate on
    offense and defense when they come up to run the
    drill again.

Inside drills

*Specialized Drill 8: Low Post Jumper or Pitch-off
(Two-on-Two)*

The position of the players in Figure 12 might leave the im-
pression that Drill 8 will be a standard two-on-two inside drill.

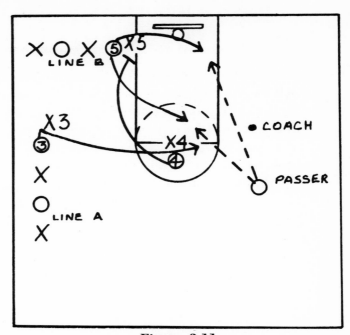

Figure 3-11
Specialized Drill 7-B
Three Man Across (with defense)
Alternative Move for 0-5

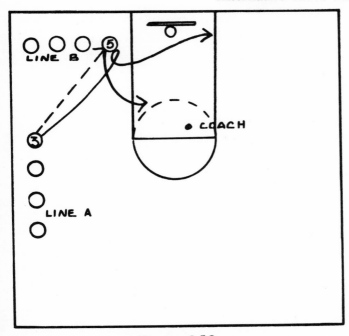

Figure 3-12
Specialized Drill 8-A
Low Post Jumper or Pitch-off
(without defense)

What makes it specialized is that the moves of the wing man and the low post man in this drill are the very same moves that these two players will make in the *Low Post Jumper or Pitch-off* option. It will be extremely valuable to you in your practice sessions since it covers key moves of the Inside Attack that must be mastered before intensive pattern work is begun. Run the drill without the defense to begin with, stressing screens, timing, and shooting. Then, as it is run with the defense, you will be able to evaluate the players' moves in relation to the defensive tactics and quickly pick out weak areas that will require more work. As you teach the drill to the players, you should emphasize the following points to the wing men:

1. Proper execution of the right type of pass (right or left hand bounce pass or overhead pass).
2. Timing.
3. Setting the right type of rolling reverse screen.
4. Staying alert for the possible pitch-off from low post after the screen is set.

Techniques for the low post men to concentrate on include:

1. Moving to get open to receive the pass in case of an overplaying defense.
2. Timing.
3. Coming over the screen properly.
4. Knowing the position of the defense.
5. Being under control on the jumper.
6. Making the correct pitch-off pass.

PROCEDURE

A. Without defense (Figure 12)
   1. The squad is divided into two groups. Line A forms behind the wing position, and Line B forms behind the low post position.

2. 0-3 passes the ball to 0-5, using the overhead pass or the right- or left-hand bounce pass. He moves to the inside of 0-5, setting a rolling screen, then continues toward the basket. 0-5 comes over the top of 0-3's screen and is now in position for his jumper over the screen.

3. Players go to the end of their own lines, and the drill continues until each player has gone through the line five times.

B. With defense (no diagram)

1. Alignment is the same as in Drill 8-A except that the first man in each line will play defense and the second man offense.

2. Procedure is like that of Drill 8-A with one addition. If the defense switches after 0-5 has come over 0-3's screen with the ball, 0-5 has the option of pitching off to 0-3, who now has excellent position on the defense under the basket.

3. All four players go to the end of their own lines; the players will alternate on offense and defense as the lines turn over.

Specialized Drill 9: Inside Post Drill

Although this last specialized drill does not cover a specific option as such, it is a very important one for the post men because it simulates moves that they may have occasion to make as they run the pattern. Low post, in particular, benefits from this drill, because on the inside options he is often in a position where he must make a quick decision as to the best way to maneuver for the ball or with the ball in order to score. The main objectives of the drill are:

1. To acquaint the post men with various inside moves.
2. To give them experience in working together.

3. To improve their overall quickness and agility.
4. To work on screening.
5. To stress ball-handling quickness.
6. To encourage them to make the strong, aggressive move to the basket.

The drill can be run in three different ways: with a basic man-to-man defense, with a switching man-to-man defense, and with a one-on-one situation for low post.

PROCEDURE

A. With basic man-to-man defense (Figure 13)
   1. Divide the post men into two lines. Line A forms behind the high post position, and Line B forms behind the low post position. The players will alternate on offense and defense in their own lines. The coach sets up at a guard position with the ball and begins the drill on the command of the whistle.
   2. 0-4 moves to set a screen for 0-5. 0-5 comes over the screen, looking for the pass from the outside guard. 0-5 receives the pass and is now free to maneuver either for the layup or jumper.
   3. After all players have played both offense and defense in their own line, the lines exchange positions and the drill continues until the players have played all positions in both lines.

B. With switching man-to-man defense (Figure 14)

   The procedure will be the same as in Drill 9-A except that 0-5 will have to adjust to the switching defense. Figure 14 shows one adjustment he can make in this situation. He has anticipated the switch and reverses back behind X-5 and comes to the ball. X-5 is waiting to pick up 0-4 and is not ready for this adjustment.

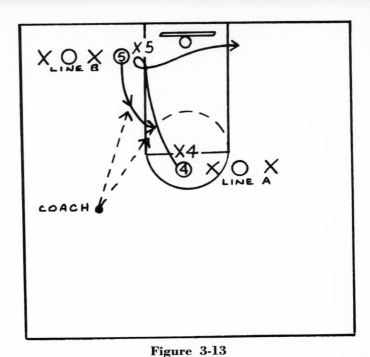

Figure 3-13
Specialized Drill 9-A
Inside Post Drill
(with basic man-to-man defense)

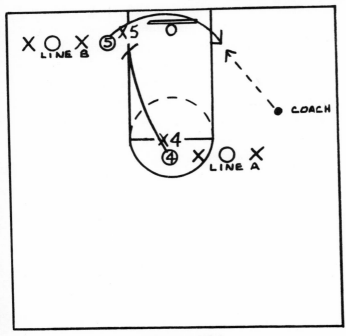

Figure 3-14
Specialized Drill 9-B
Inside Post Drill
(with switching man-to-man defense)

C. With one-on-one (no diagram)

1. The alignment and rotation are the same as in Drills 9-A and 9-B.

2. 0-4 receives the pass from the coach, pivots to the inside, and fronts the basket, holding the ball high in the air. 0-5 now has the responsibility of whipping X-5 on a one-on-one. 0-5 makes his move, receives the ball from 0-4, and maneuvers with his own individual moves for the basket. Emphasis is placed here on 0-5 making a strong move to the basket.

Selected basic drills

When specialized drills, like the ones described in the first part of this chapter, are used in practice sessions, there will be no need to utilize a full slate of basic offensive drills in addition. The specialized drills contain many of the fundamental techniques that ordinarily must be covered by a number of separate offensive drills (and defensive drills as well). However, there will be times when you will want to round out your practice session with some basic drills that stress specific skills. The following basic drills have been especially selected to accompany the specialized pattern drills for use with the Multiple-Continuous Offense. No procedure will be given for the first five drills, because most coaches are familiar with them already and use them in their daily practices. The last four drills, which may not be so widely used, are given in detail.

Basic Drill 1: FIGURE EIGHT (half and whole court)

Basic Drill 2: LAYUPS (right-hand layups, left-hand layups, and front-of-the-rim layups, with and without use of the board)

Basic Drill 3: MAN IN THE MIDDLE

Basic Drill 4: GIVE AND GO

Basic Drill 5: STANDARD PASSING DRILL (stressing all kinds of passes)

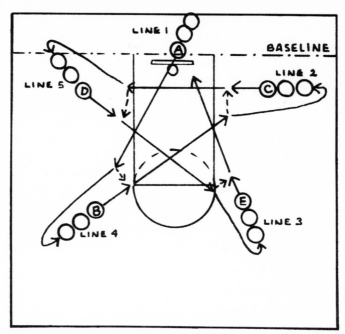

Figure 3-15
Basic Drill 6—Star Pep Drill

Basic Drill 6: Star Pep Drill (Figure 15)

Drill 6 stresses passing on the move. The three types of passes that should be used with this drill are the left-hand bounce pass, the right-hand bounce pass, and the two-handed push bounce pass. Techniques which should be kept in mind by the players as they run the drill include (1) keeping the ball low, (2) keeping the body low and under control, and (3) timing. The players will take pride in running the drill at full speed for as long as possible without making a mistake.

PROCEDURE

1. The squad is divided into five groups which form lines as indicated in Figure 15.
2. The drill is begun by A, who has the ball. He dribbles toward Line 4 and passes the ball to B, who has moved up from his line to receive the pass. A goes to the end of Line 4, and B moves with the ball toward Line 2,

passes to C, and goes to the end of Line 2. The drill continues with C passing to D, D passing to E, and E passing to the next man up in Line 1, etc.

Basic Drill 7: Star Shooting Drill (no diagram)

Drill 7 is somewhat different from the standard shooting drills which usually have the players shooting right- and left-hand layups from the sides or over-the-rim shots from the top of the key. It is a very valuable passing and shooting drill which will improve (1) floor position shooting, (2) reaction time, (3) quickness, and (4) body control.

PROCEDURE

This drill is set up and begun in the same manner as Drill 6. Then, when the coach blows his whistle, the player with the ball becomes the shooter. He takes his shot from whatever position he is in when he hears the whistle. Then the drill picks up where it left off until the whistle is blown again and another player takes a shot. Besides learning to shoot spontaneously, the players gain experience in trying for jumpers and layups on the move from all over the court.

Basic Drill 8: Board Tip Drill (Figure 16)

Techniques to be stressed in this drill include (1) staying on the balls of the feet; (2) keeping the eyes on the ball; (3) keeping the arm extended; (4) using the fingers and wrist, not the full hand; (5) timing; and (6) quickness and coordination.

PROCEDURE

1. Divide the squad into two lines. Place the lines in the positions indicated in Figure 16.
2. Give a ball to the first player in each line and have him tip the ball right-handed against the backboard at basket level ten times in succession. When he completes his tips, the second player moves up and begins

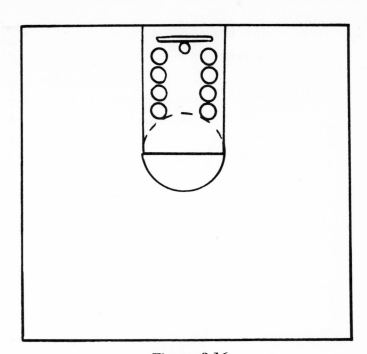

Figure 3-16
Basic Drill 8—Board Tip Drill

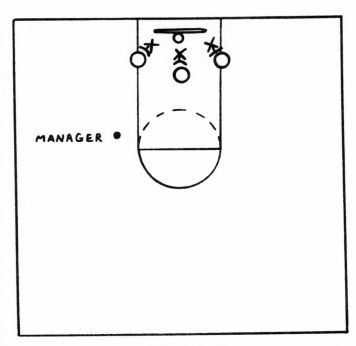

MANAGER ●

Figure 3-17
Basic Drill 9
Competitive Rebounding Drill

his tips, coordinating his move so that the rhythm of the tips is constant during the switch.

3. When all players have completed their turn using the right-hand tip, the drill is repeated with the left-hand tip, and then again using alternating right-hand and left-hand tips.

Basic Drill 9: Competitive Rebounding Drill
(Figure 17)

Although many coaches feel that rebounding drills are of value to the inside big men only, rebounding positioning should be taught as an automatic reaction to all members of the team. Many times in a game situation the post man will take a shot from eight or ten feet out, leaving a smaller man in a position where he must attempt to rebound despite the height disadvantage.

Drill 9 covers both the offensive and defensive phases of rebounding. Points that should be stressed to the players for both phases are (1) knowing from what position on the floor the shot is taken; (2) making a *strong* move to the board, jumping and timing the ball properly; (3) controlling the ball, once it is taken, with good body balance and with a firm grip; (4) aggressiveness. Specific techniques to be taught as the players alternate on offense and defense are as follows:

Offense: 1. The step-around move (right or left).
        2. The tip back (out) technique.
        3. Use of the body to cause the defensive man to lose his balance and control.
        4. Use of the body to force the defensive man way in, away from his regular position.

Defense: 1. Maintenance of the defensive position between the offensive man and the basket.
        2. The turn, as the ball is shot, with emphasis on keeping the offensive player at his back.

3. Body position on the turn—keeping legs spread and using the arms and hands as he turns (not as a holding-back maneuver but in order to feel pressure).
4. Determination of offensive man's position when pressure is felt.

PROCEDURE

1. Three defensive players form a semicircle two or three feet from the basket; their backs are to the basket. Three offensive players line up in front of the defensive players.
2. As the manager shoots the ball from different areas of the floor, all six players go for the rebound. The defense receives one point for each rebound they get; the offense receives a point for each ball they rebound. The drill is run until a total of five, ten, or fifteen points (depending on how much time is to be spent on the drill) is reached. Then the players reverse on offense and defense and play another game of five, ten, or fifteen.
3. As soon as the first six players complete both phases of the drill, six new players move into position and the drill is continued.

4

The Outside Attack of the M-C Pattern

Every coach knows that he must have a well-balanced attack in order to win consistently. Not only is balance a necessity in order to be a winner; it also helps to control the ever-existing problem of keeping the defense honest. At the same time, it gives the outside guards and the wing man the feeling that they are as important in the offensive makeup as the often overemphasized big-man-inside factor. The time is gone when one outstanding man (big or small) can win for you in high school basketball. The players now are extremely accurate in shooting set shots and jumpers, and they are much more skilled in shooting jumpers on the move and using both hands while driving layups than they have been in years past. As a result, winning teams must have well-balanced scoring from both the outside and the inside players. This means that your outside shooters must hit in the area of 48 per cent plus from the field, while your inside men should be capable of shooting a 52 per cent average or better.

An essential ingredient of a balanced offensive pattern is a strong outside attack. The goal of the Outside Attack of the Multiple-Continuous Offense is to gain good balanced floor position shots and jumpers for the outside men from the top of the circle (doll's head) to the corners as indicated by the shaded area in Figure 1. The outside players have a choice of two ways in which to begin the Outside Attack—(1) the *Give and Go Variation* and (2) the *Basic Give and Go*. The other outside options of the pattern (with the exception of a planned *Big Man—Little Man Switch*) are run as a continuation of one or the other of these two plays.

Give and go variation (Figures 2, 3, 4)

A variation of the *Basic Give and Go* is the first option you look for from the pattern when using the Outside Attack. Its

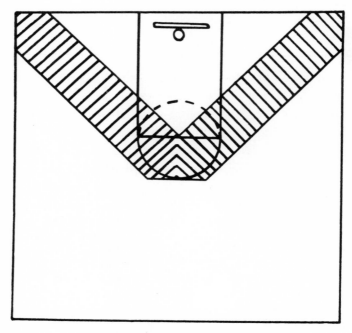

Figure 4-1
General Area of Outside Attack

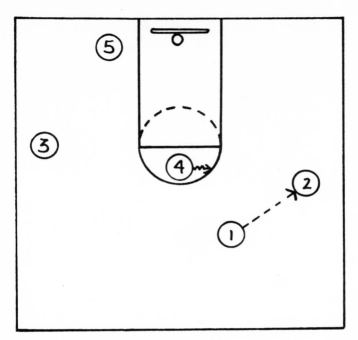

Figure 4-2
Give and Go Variation (1)

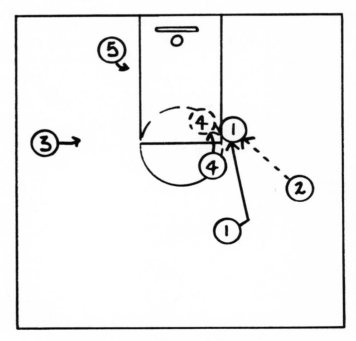

Figure 4-3
Give and Go Variation (2)

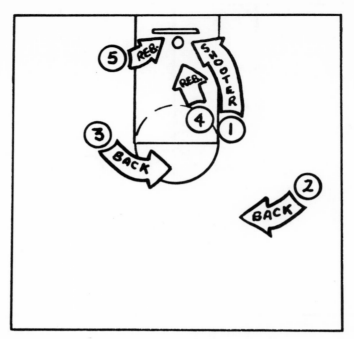

Figure 4-4
Give and Go Variation (3)

setup is slightly different from the normal give and go that most coaches use in that the post man (4) always screens for the give and go man (1). You begin the pattern with 1 passing the ball to 2. Then 4 takes a lateral step toward the ball to help set up a pick (screen) for 1 (Figure 2). 1 takes a step toward 2 (the ball man) as though he intends to set a screen for 2, but then he makes a direct cut for the basket over 4's screen and receives the pass from 2 (Figure 3). 1 has the option of going all the way to the basket for a layup, or in many situations (depending on how the defense reacts) he can pull up for a quick jumper (Figure 4). This will put the pressure on the defense; the inside defensive man will foul 1 frequently as he makes his move to the basket. 4 and 5, after seeing the option work, move into rebounding position; 3 drops back with 2 to maintain fast-break defensive balance. If 1 does not get the return pass from 2, he swings out and sets up in the corner.

This option is keyed by 1's motion in the direction of the basket after his pass to 2; that move sets it up.

Player Responsibilities

1 passes to 2. After the pass he steps toward 2 as if to screen, and then he turns and cuts to the basket across 4's screen. He receives the pass from 2 and pulls up for a jumper or goes in for a layup. If the second pass from 2 fails to materialize, he goes to the corner.

2 receives the initial pass from 1 and throws back to 1 as 1 moves to the basket. He then remains outside for defensive responsibility.

3 releases back to the top of the key to the fast break defensive position when 1 shoots the ball.

4 takes a lateral step toward 1 to set a screen after 1's pass to 2. As the pass is made back to 1, he goes in for the rebound.

5 rebounds.

Three man across (Figures 5, 6, 7)

If 2 fails to get the pass back to 1 in the *Give and Go Variation,* the pattern automatically shifts into the *Three Man Across.* As 1 goes to the corner, 4 turns and starts his move away from the ball (Figure 5), hesitating to screen for the 3 man. 3 fakes to the baseline with one step, comes back off the screen set by 4, and continues on through, looking for the pass from 2 any time after he has passed the screen (Figure 6). 2 times 3's move and passes the ball in for a layup or a pullup jumper (Figure 7). 3, 4, and 5 are on the inside to rebound, and 1 and 2 move back to the fast break defensive balance positions.

Player responsibilities

1 gets his position in the corner, and then as 3 shoots, slides back to the fast-break outlet position.

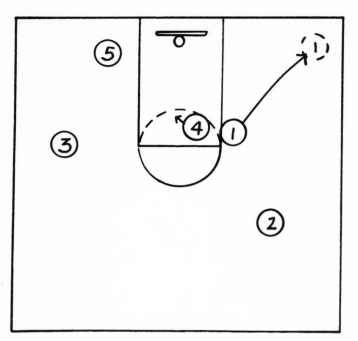

Figure 4-5
Three Man Across (1)

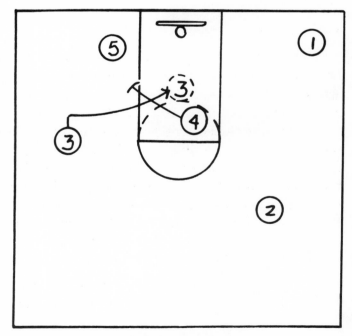

Figure 4-6
Three Man Across (2)

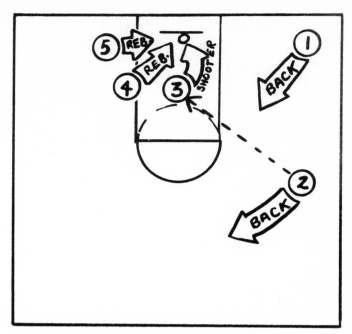

Figure 4-7
Three Man Across (3)

2 has the ball, watches for 3 to cross 4's screen, and passes the ball to 3 as he comes through. 2 then drops back for defensive coverage.

3 takes one step (faking to the baseline) and then turns and moves across 4's screen and receives the pass from 2. He takes a pullup jumper or goes in for a layup.

4 moves away from the ball to the basket and screens for 3 as 3 goes through. He helps rebound.

5 rebounds.

One to three (Figures 8, 9, 10)

Here is a second option that relies on the wing man (3). You move right into this option if 2 is unable to hit the wing man in the *Three Man Across*. When 3 fails to receive the ball from 2, he sets up low opposite the 5 man. 2 makes his pass to 1 in the corner (Figure 8). 1 looks for 3, who now has a one-on-one in or around the basket area. 1 passes the ball to 3, who

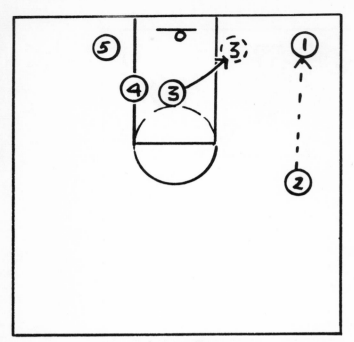

Figure 4-8
One to Three (1)

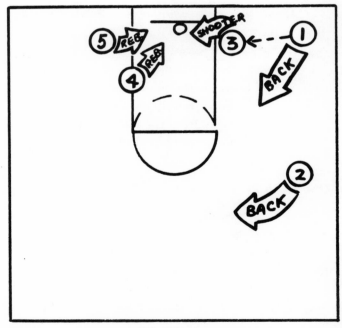

Figure 4-9
One to Three (2)

already has position on his defensive man for a turn-around jumper (Figure 9). 3 has the option of shooting or of passing off to 5, who has moved out from low post (Figure 10). If 3 shoots, 4 and 5 will rebound. The pass from 1 to 3 has to be a quick pass; any delay in the movement of the offense will eliminate this option since the defense will have time to adjust.

Player responsibilities

1 receives the ball from 2, passes to 3, and then drops back for defensive balance as 3 shoots the ball.

2 passes the ball to 1 in the corner and moves back for defensive coverage.

3 moves in low and receives the pass from 1. He has a turn-around jumper or he can pass off to 5.

4 rebounds.

5 watches for possible pass from 3 for a layup or rebounds.

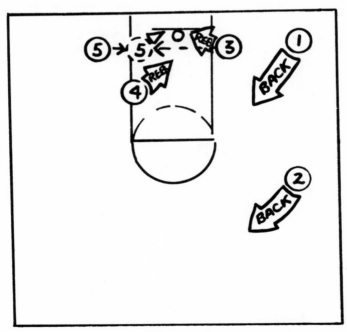

Figure 4-10
One to Three (3)

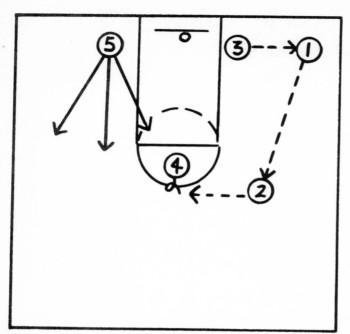

Figure 4-11
Five Up (1)

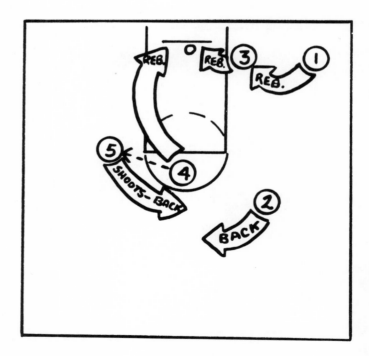

Figure 4-12
Five Up (2)

Five up (Figures 11, 12, 13)

Sometimes during the course of the game (especially against zone defenses) neither 1 nor 3 will be able to obtain a good shot from the preceding options. When this happens, the offense can take advantage of the overload that is developed by the *Three Man Across* with the use of the *Five Up* option. In Figure 11, while the ball is being passed from 3 to 1 and back outside again to 2, 5 is moving up from his low post position to the area of the free-throw line extended. 2 can either throw the ball directly to 5 or pass to 4, who will pull out to get the ball. 4 passes to 5 (Figure 12), and 5 may either maneuver for a jumper or he can pitch off to 1 or to 3, who may be open if the defense shifts toward the ball man (Figure 13). As 5 receives the ball, 4 moves to the inside, resulting in a temporary exchange of positions between 4 and 5.

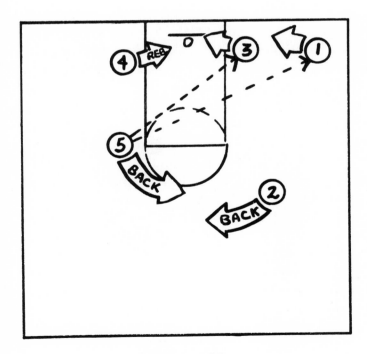

Figure 4-13
Five Up (3)

Player responsibilities

1 receives the ball from 3, passes to 2, and stays alert for a possible pitch-off from 5 or rebounds.

2 receives pass from 1, either passes to 4 or directly to 5, and remains outside for defensive coverage.

3 passes to 1 and receives pitch-off from 5 or rebounds.

4 pulls out to receive the ball from 2 and passes to 5. He then moves toward the low post position for the rebound.

5 pulls up to the area of the free-throw line extended as the ball is being moved around the outside. He receives the pass from either 2 or 4 and takes a jumper or pitches off to 1 or to 3. In either case, he then drops back to the fast-break defensive balance position.

Basic give and go (Figures 14, 15, 16)

The second way to begin the Outside Attack is by using the *Basic Give and Go*. In Figure 14, the 1 man again keys the option; when he passes to 2 and does not move, 2 knows he should work the *Basic Give and Go* rather than the *Variation*. 2 returns the pass to 1, fakes to screen for 1, and then heads toward the basket (Figure 15). 4 knows not to take the lateral screen for 1 and stays at the top of the key in order to give 1 and 2 more room in which to work. In Figure 16, 2 receives the pass from 1 and has the option of going all the way for a layup or of pulling up with the ball for a quick jumper if the defense has clogged up the middle. The second pass from 1 to 2 must be a quick pass rather than a bounce pass, due to the proximity of the defensive players. The 4 and 5 men are inside to rebound, while 1 is back on defense. 3 slides back to the top of the key for fast-break defensive balance position. If 2 does not get the pass from 1, he continues on through; this move sets up the *Outside Reverse*.

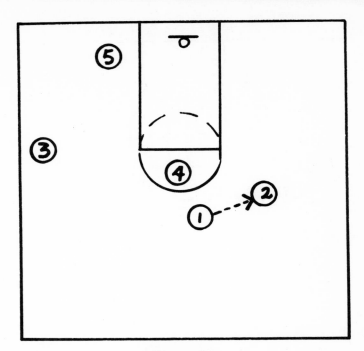

Figure 4-14
Basic Give and Go (1)

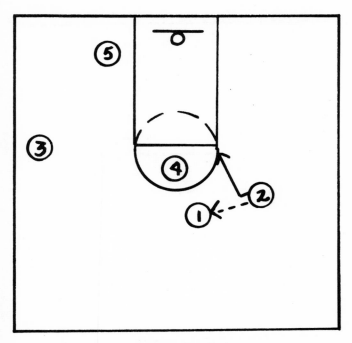

Figure 4-15
Basic Give and Go (2)

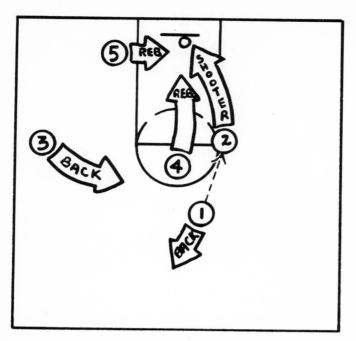

Figure 4-16
Basic Give and Go (3)

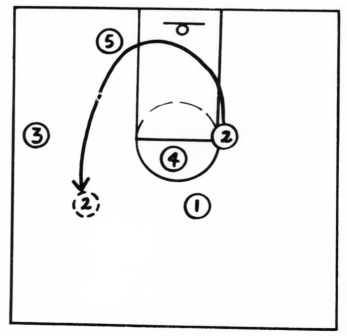

Figure 4-17
Outside Reverse (1)

Player responsibilities

1 passes to 2 and remains in position to receive the
   return pass from 2. He throws the ball back to 2 as 2
   moves toward the basket and then backs up to his
   outside defensive position.
2 receives the initial pass from 1, returns the ball to 1,
   and steps toward 1 as if to screen. He then makes a cut
   to the basket, receiving the ball on the move from 1.
   He goes in for a layup or pulls up for a jumper. If the
   second pass from 1 does not materialize, he clears and
   goes through.
3 slides back to the top of key for balance.
4 and 5 rebound.

Outside reverse (Figures 17, 18, 19)

When the 2 man makes his move to the basket in the preceding option and the give and go is not there, 1 shifts to the
Outside Reverse. In Figure 17, 2 has cleared, gone through,
and is now outside again to the left of 1. When 2 gets his position, 1 starts his move, looking for 4 to help him. 1 drops his
defensive man over the top of 4's screen, uses the reverse
dribble, and heads for the basket as shown in Figure 18. 1 has
the option of going all the way with the ball for a layup or of
pulling up for a quick jumper at the top of the key before the
defense can switch. 4 and 5 go to the basket to rebound; 3
slides back to the top of the key, and the 2 man moves to his
fast-break defensive position (Figure 19).

Player responsibilities

1 holds up with the ball until 2 goes through. Then he
   loses his defensive man on 4's screen, reverse dribbles,
   and heads for the basket with the ball. He either pulls
   up for a jumper or takes the ball in for a layup.

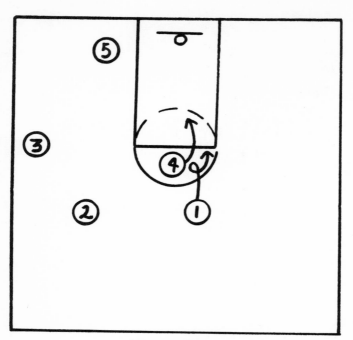

Figure 4-18
Outside Reverse (2)

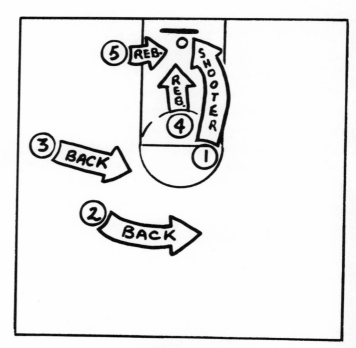

Figure 4-19
Outside Reverse (3)

2 clears and comes through to the opposite side to take up the defensive responsibility as 1 moves to the basket.

3 slides to the top of the key for fast-break defensive balance.

4 sets a screen for 1's reverse and goes on in for the rebound.

5 rebounds.

Big man—little man switch (Figures 20, 21, 22, 23)

The perfect situation in basketball is an offensive setup which causes the defense to switch, with a 6' guard playing a 6'4" post man and a 6'4" or 6'5" post man playing a 5'10" or 6' guard. This is one situation that all coaches, regardless of the type of offense they use, always strive to get at one time or another during a ball game. Often it will develop as a result of screens or other unforeseen moves. On the other hand, many coaches will create this switch as an integral phase of their offensive attack and will use it as a special weapon when and if they need it. When the switch occurs, the offense must be ready to take advantage of it before the defensive players can adjust and move back to their original assignments.

Creating the Switch

If you plan to create the switch, it should be keyed during a time out. You begin by having the 2 man clear (Figure 20) so that the right side of the court will be free for the maneuvers of 1 and 4. The objective of the 1 man is to put his defensive man into a position that will keep him from picking up 1 on the reverse. 1 starts his move with the ball by taking his defensive man to the right outside shoulder of 4; then he makes his reverse back from the overload side and heads in the direction of the corner with the ball as shown in Figure 21. This usually causes the defense to switch, with 4's defensive man

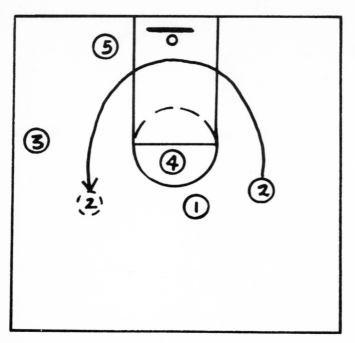

Figure 4-20
Big Man—Little Man
Switch (1)

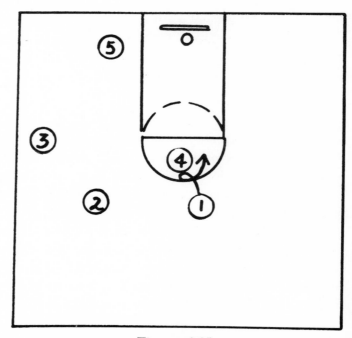

Figure 4-21
Big Man—Little Man
Switch (2)

(a big man) having to play 1 and 1's defensive man (a little man) playing 4. 4 now moves toward the basket, receives the ball from 1, and goes in for the field goal (Figure 22). He will be fouled about 75 per cent of the time and can get a two- or three-point play from this purposely planned defensive switch. 5 comes in to rebound, and 2 and 3 are outside for defensive coverage.

If the switch does not occur, 1 can go ahead and go in for the layup; if he is picked up low by the inside defensive man, he can pitch off to the low offensive man (5) for a layup (Figure 23).

Player responsibilities

1 waits for 2 to clear. Then he drops his defensive man on 4 and reverses to the right side of the court toward the basket. If the defensive switch is made, he passes the ball to 4 and helps rebound; if it is not made, he goes in with the ball for a layup or pulls up and passes off to 5 and helps rebound.

2 clears and goes through and remains outside.

3 drops back for defensive coverage.

4 screens for 1 and then slides toward the basket to receive the pass from 1 for a shot. If the switch fails, he goes in for the rebound.

5 rebounds. If the switch is not made, he watches for the possible pass from 1 for a layup.

The Unplanned Switch

The *Big Man–Little Man Switch* may occur spontaneously as 1 prepares to return the ball to 2 on the *Basic Give and Go.* If the outside men see that the defense has switched and a small man is playing 4, then 2 clears quickly and 1 takes the ball in and passes off to 4 for the basket. It is essential that the players be watching for this situation to develop so that they can take full advantage of it before the defense realizes what

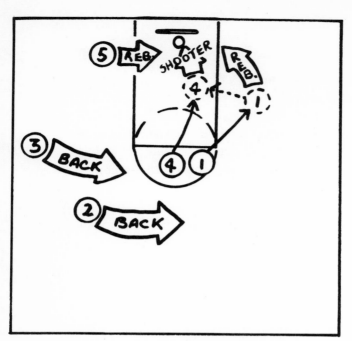

Figure 4-22
Big Man—Little Man
Switch (3)

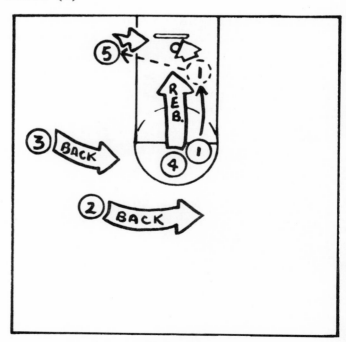

Figure 4-23
Big Man—Little Man
Switch (4)

is happening. Player responsibilities will be the same as if the switch were a planned one.

In conclusion, it is evident that the 1 man is the playmaker for the Outside Attack. He can begin the pattern with the *Give and Go Variation* or the *Basic Give and Go,* or he can run the *Big Man—Little Man Switch.* On the other hand, even though 1 begins the plays, the talents of 2 and 3 are equally important to the attack. As the pattern shifts from one option to another, 1, 2, and 3 are each designated as the shooter in at least one option:

Give and Go ➤ *Three Man* ➤ *One to Three* ➤ *Five Up*
Variation   *Across*   (Shooter is   (Shooter is
(Shooter is 1) (Shooter is 3) 3 or 5)   5, 1, or 3)

Basic Give and Go   ➤   *Outside Reverse*
(Shooter is 2)   (Shooter is 1)

Big Man—Little Man Switch   (Shooter is 1 or 5 if
(Shooter is 4 if switch is made) ➤ switch is not made)

Proper utilization of these options of the Multiple-Continuous pattern, along with a maximum of work, patience, and planning, will give you a strong outside attack. Your players should be able to run these outside options so automatically that there will be no question in their minds about what to do if one option doesn't work out. Much of the success of the options depends on the ability of the offense to move quickly in order to throw the defense off balance. The continuity inherent in the pattern will be effective only if it is executed smoothly and fluidly with no hesitation or confusion. Then you will be able to relieve much of the pressure that ordinarily falls on the inside offensive men, thus making your offense stronger and more respected by the defense.

5

The Inside Attack of the M-C Pattern

The Inside Attack of the Multiple-Continuous Offense is designed to utilize the skills and ability of the wing man, the low post man, and the high post man. It is used in the area between the free-throw line extended and the baseline (the shaded area in Figure 1). This area will give players 3, 4, and 5 plenty of room in which to maneuver.

You will want to use all of the options of the Inside Attack at the beginning of the game so that you can quickly determine the weaknesses of your opponent. By running every option you will cause a certain amount of switching, and you will be able to pick out the poor defensive player or players almost immediately. You can then begin the Inside Attack in earnest, concentrating on the use of one option geared to the poorest defensive player. If your opponent should call time out and change defensive assignments or make adjustments, you can go ahead and run the other options, always concentrating on a definite option and ever conscious of looking for the weak defensive man.

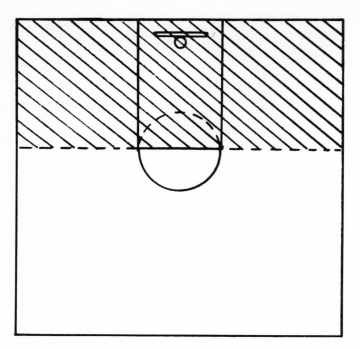

Figure 5-1
Area of Inside Attack

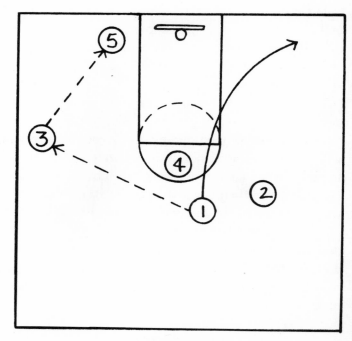

Figure 5-2
Key to Inside Attack

The Inside Attack is begun by 1 passing the ball to 3 and going through to the corner opposite the ball. You now have a two-on-two situation, and the wing man (3) and the post man (5) have plenty of room in which to work. 3 then passes the ball to 5 and heads toward the opposite low post position (Figure 2). Those two passes are the key to the options of the Inside Attack.

Inside give and go (Figures 3, 4)

In Figure 3, 3 receives the ball from 1, passes to 5, fakes to the middle, and heads for the goal. 5 returns the ball to 3 for a basket any time after 3 begins his move (Figure 4). 4 and 5 come in to rebound, and 2 remains outside for defensive coverage. 1 slides back to the top of the key area for back-court balance and pattern turnover.

This option will not always be successful, but during the course of the game it should produce several baskets if the defense is not doing its job; any slack on the part of the defensive man or any mistake he makes on this option will result in a basket. If 5 fails to return the ball to 3, 3 sets up near the baseline in the low post position opposite the ball; this will create a one-on-one with 5 and his defensive man.

Player responsibilities

1 passes to 3 and goes through to the opposite corner. As the ball is put on the boards, he moves back for defensive coverage.

2 remains outside for balance.

3 receives the ball from 1, passes to 5, fakes to the middle, and begins his cut to the basket. He gets the pass from 5 and goes in for a layup or pulls up for a jumper. If he does not receive the return pass from 5, he sets up at the opposite low post in rebounding position.

4 rebounds.

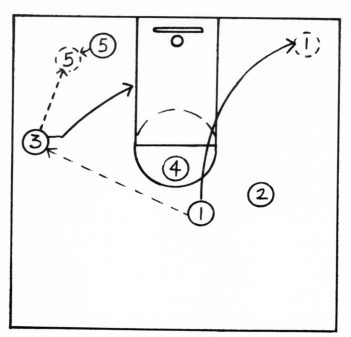

Figure 5-3
Inside Give and Go (1)

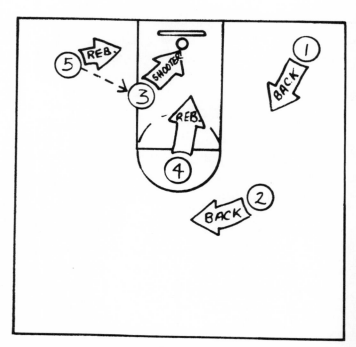

Figure 5-4
Inside Give and Go (2)

5 pulls out to receive the pass from 3, returns the ball to 3, and goes in for the rebound.

Low post jumper or pitch-off (Figures 5, 6)

In Figure 5, the wing man (3) has received the ball from 1 and passes to 5. As 3 goes through after the pass, he sets a screen for 5; he then goes through to the opposite low post. 5 immediately moves off the screen and goes up for a quick jumper. 3 and 4 rebound; 1 slides back to the top of the key to maintain defensive balance; and 2 again remains outside.

If 5 sees that he cannot get off his shot as he goes up for the jumper, he has the option to pitch off to 3 (Figure 6). If the defense switches, this option will work because 3 is on the inside of 5's defensive man and has a good shooting position. 4 and 5 will rebound, 2 remains outside, and 1 slides back to the top of the key for defensive balance.

Player responsibilities

1 passes to 3 and goes through to the corner. He then moves back to the top of the key as the ball is shot.

2 remains outside.

3 receives the ball from 1 and passes to 5. He fakes to the baseline and then goes through to the opposite low post. He screens for 5 as he goes through and then watches for the possible pitch-off from 5 for a basket.

4 rebounds.

5 pulls out to receive the ball from 3, moves across 3's screen, and goes up for a quick jumper or goes up and pitches off to 3 and helps rebound.

Two man through (Figures 7, 8)

If 5 is checked as he comes off 3's screen for his jumper, 2 automatically moves off 4's screen and heads for the basket (Figure 7). 5 passes the ball to 2 any time after 2 passes the screen, and 2 goes all the way in for a layup (Figure 8). If

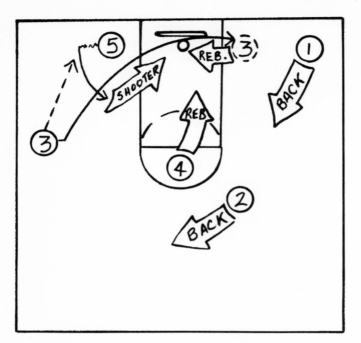

Figure 5-5
Low Post Jumper or Pitch-off (1)

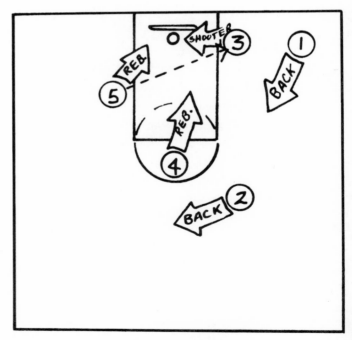

Figure 5-6
Low Post Jumper or Pitch-off (2)

the defense has dropped off on the inside, 2 can pull up for a quick 10-12 foot jumper. 3 and 5 are in perfect rebounding position to form a fence under the basket, and 4 drops back to the top of the key. 1 slides from the corner back outside for defensive balance.

This option is tough to cover because the ball is inside, and many high school defensive players will have a tendency to take their eyes off their man and turn toward the inside. This gives 2 a chance to make his move while the defense is off guard.

Player responsibilities

1 moves back outside for defensive coverage as 2 comes through.

2 moves across 4's screen, receives the ball from 5, and goes in for the layup or pulls up for a jumper.

3 rebounds.

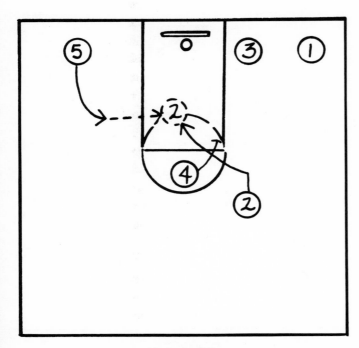

Figure 5-7
Two Man Through (1)

4 sets the screen for 2 and then drops back to the top of
the key.

5 passes the ball to 2 as he comes through and helps
rebound.

Back door or pitch-out (Figures 9, 10)

In Figure 9, 1 passes to 3 and goes to the corner. 3 passes to
5, looks for the give and go, and sets up at low post opposite
the ball, keying on 5's move. 5 pulls out to receive the pass; he
then turns and maneuvers his defensive man along the baseline
toward the basket. In Figure 10, 3 immediately pulls out
toward the free-throw line, and if 5 is double-teamed or otherwise cannot get off a shot, he can pitch out to 3 or to 4 for a
basket. If 5 shoots, 3 and 4 will rebound. If 5 pitches off, he and
either 3 or 4 (depending on who receives the pitch-off) will
rebound. In either case, 1 and 2 will drop back to maintain
defensive balance.

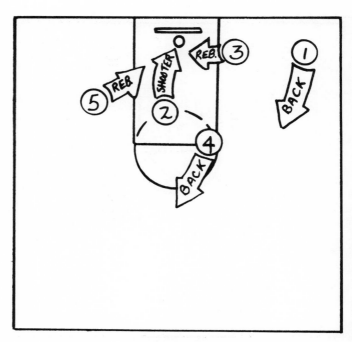

Figure 5-8
Two Man Through (2)

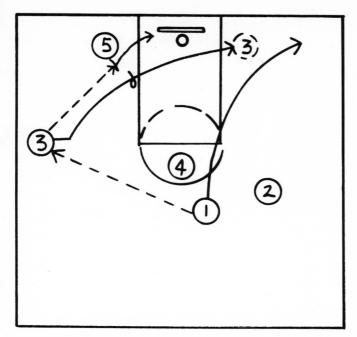

Figure 5-9
Back Door or Pitch-out (1)

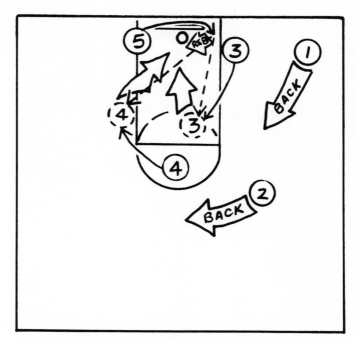

Figure 5-10
Back Door or Pitch-out (2)

Player responsibilities

1 passes to 3 and goes to the corner. As the ball is put on the boards, he slides back to the top of the key.

2 remains outside.

3 moves out to receive the ball from 1, passes to 5, and goes through to the opposite low post. Then he moves out toward the free-throw line to receive the possible pitch-out from 5 for a basket or he helps rebound.

4 moves toward the basket to receive the possible pass from 5 for a shot and/or helps rebound.

5 pulls out to receive the pass from 3, maneuvers along the baseline for a shot or pitches out to 3 or 4 and then rebounds.

Three man around (Figures 11, 12)

This is the last option of the Inside Attack. It is used any time during the course of the game when the offense is going for the "one shot." After receiving the ball from 1, 3 passes to 5 and then sets a moving screen all the way through and pulls up at the low post opposite 5. 5 pulls out to receive the pass from 3 and fronts the basket (Figure 11). As soon as 5 makes his move, 4 rolls back to screen for 3. 3 comes off 4's screen looking for the pass from 5 for a basket (Figure 12). 4 and 5 rebound, 2 pulls back to the outside for balance, and 1 slides back to the top of the key.

If the play is executed and timed properly, 3 will have a left-handed layup or a quick three-foot jumper in front of the basket. An added advantage of this option is the fact that 5 has a one-on-one situation; if his defensive man drops off to cover 3, 5 can take a 10 foot jumper from the side.

Player responsibilities

1 passes to 3, goes to the corner, then slides back to the top of the key for defensive balance.

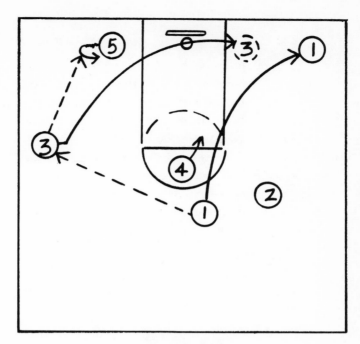

Figure 5-11
Three Man Around (1)

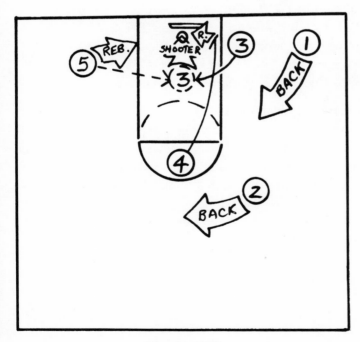

Figure 5-12
Three Man Around (2)

2 pulls back outside.

3 receives the ball from 1, passes to 5, and screens for 5 on the way to the opposite low post position. Then he turns, rolls off 4's screen, receives the pass from 5, and goes in for the basket.

4 screens for 3 as 3 comes around and helps rebound.

5 pulls out to receive the ball from 3, turns toward the basket, passes the ball to 3, and rebounds. (If 3 is double-teamed, 5 takes a jumper from the side.)

In conclusion, it is obvious that player 5 on low post is the "head man" of the Inside Attack. After 1 and 3 get the ball to him, it is he who decides which option to run. Depending on the defensive setup, he can make any one of the following moves:

1. Pass to 3 as 3 goes through (*Inside Give and Go*)
2. Move off 3's screen for a jumper, or
3. Go up for the jumper but pitch off to 3 (*Low Post Jumper* or *Pitch-off*)
4. Pass to 2 for a layup (*Two Man Through*)
5. Maneuver along the baseline for a shot, or
6. Pitch out to 3 or 4 (*Back Door* or *Pitch-out*)
7. Run the "one shot" option (*Three Man Around*)

The 3 man will always begin his move toward the opposite low post after his pass to 5. Otherwise, after 5 receives the ball, all moves by the other four offensive players are keyed by what 5 does. As in the Outside Attack, your players must be able to run the inside options automatically and be prepared to move from one option to another quickly in order to preserve the continuity of the pattern. Only then will you have a strong Inside Attack.

6

Combating Zone Defenses with the M-C Offense

In the last few years the offensive ability of both high school and college basketball players has improved tremendously. Coaches are often heard to make the comment that, as in football, the offensive phase of basketball is much more advanced than the defensive phase. As a result, there has been an organized and concentrated effort all over the country to improve and refine defensive tactics. It is no longer possible to plan an offensive attack without taking into consideration how effective it will be against the many types of defenses now in existence. Even though your team may be taller and stronger and possess better shooters than a given opponent, you may end up on the short end of the final score if you are not prepared to combat the particular defensive system he chooses to use against you.

The Multiple-Continuous Offense will serve you well against all types of defense. However, no offense is infallible; it is most important that you have an idea of what to expect from each commonly used zone and man-to-man defense in the actual game situation. Then you will be able to plan your game strategy accordingly, devising the best possible attack against each defense that is likely to be encountered, in view of your particular circumstances. Chapters 6 and 7 were designed for just this purpose—to familiarize you generally with the reaction of many types of defense to the options of the Multiple-Continuous Offense and to suggest the most effective options to use in each situation.

When a coach knows that he is likely to be facing a zone defense in a given ball game, many factors will affect his game preparation. Questions such as these will run through his mind: What type of zone will they use? Will they concentrate the defense on the inside? Will they give us the inside and force on the outside? What type of rotation will they use? Will they push the ball and play a forcing zone? Will we be allowed to set up on offense and work the ball? These are only a few of the problems with which a coach must deal as he formulates his game plans for an opponent who nearly always adheres to a zone type of defense.

Ordinarily, game strategy will be planned around the zone defense that the opponent uses most frequently. Each type of zone will require adjustments in offense maneuvers, and it is often difficult to determine which attack might be most effective against a particular zone setup. One of the strong points of the Multiple-Continuous Offense is that it will be effective against *all* zone defenses because it causes the defense to shift or to rotate differently from what it is accustomed to doing. The basic continuous movement will force the defensive players into positions where they normally do not play and will pull them away from their rebounding positions.

This chapter will cover the options that have proved most effective against each of four commonly used zone defenses: the 1-3-1, the 2-1-2, the 1-2-2, and the 2-3 zones. It will discuss in relation to each zone (1) which options to use, (2) how to use them to best advantage, and (3) what reaction to expect from the defense as the options are run. It will also suggest variations of the pattern that will provide scoring opportunities in addition to the ones basic to each option.

Attacking the 1-3-1 zone

A team that uses a 1-3-1 zone against the M-C Offense can find itself at a tremendous disadvantage. This zone has a number of weaknesses, especially in the corners and along the baseline. In many cases, the point defensive man is confronted with a double-coverage situation. Too, some coaches will have their wing man drop down to cover the corner areas and hold their baseline man in tight, which results in an extra-wide rotation area for the defensive wing men. There will be definite outside shooting areas open against this zone. Figure 1 shows the basic setup of the M-C Offense against a 1-3-1 situation.

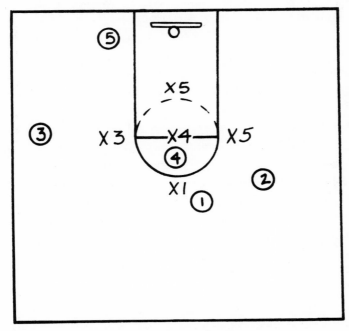

Figure 6-1
Basic Setup Against 1-3-1 Zone

Give and Go Variation (Figures 2 and 3)

The *Give and Go Variation* should be used to begin the attack. After 0-1 passes the ball to 0-2 and makes his move over 0-4's screen toward the corner, X-1 will usually move over to cover 0-2. Either X-2 will take 0-1, or X-5 will pick him up. Many times coaches will tell their back man on the 1-3-1 (X-5) that he has baseline responsibility; this being the case, X-5 moves out to cover 0-1, and X-2 splits the difference between the ball man (0-2) and 0-1 (Figure 2). Due to the concentration of defensive men in the circle area, 0-2 must ordinarily delay his pass to 0-1 until 0-1 approaches or reaches the corner. If the defense fails to react quickly, the *Give and Go* will be successful, and 0-1 will have a shot from the corner. Or, if X-1 fails to cover the initial pass from 0-1 to 0-2 in time, 0-2 can take an outside shot as soon as he receives the ball instead of working the *Give and Go*.

Another scoring possibility from this option involves 0-4. Sometimes, depending on the rotation of the defense, X-2 will pick up 0-2 after the initial pass is made, leaving X-1 to fall off and help. In this case, X-5 must pull out to cover 0-1 on his move to the corner. As 0-2 returns the pass to 0-1, 0-4 releases to the basket, with X-4 sliding with him (Figure 3). 0-1 and 0-4 both will have one-on-one situations, and if X-4 doesn't body-check 0-4 on the move to the goal, 0-1 can pass to 0-4 for a basket. Since X-3 has backside responsibility and 0-5 to consider, he is not likely to stop 0-4's move, and 0-4 has an excellent opportunity to score. The offense can pick up a number of easy baskets in this manner because the defense will let 0-4 go much of the time, concentrating their efforts on 0-1. It is very unusual for X-1 or X-2 to pick up 0-4 before he has the ball and shooting position, and his position in relation to X-5 is ideal.

As evidenced in the foregoing, the *Give and Go Variation* as utilized against a 1-3-1 has tremendous scoring potential— (1) 0-2 can shoot from his outside position, and (2) 0-1 can

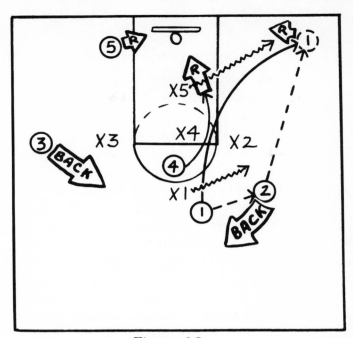

Figure 6-2
Give and Go Variation
Against 1-3-1 Zone
(Scoring opportunities for 0-1 and 0-2)

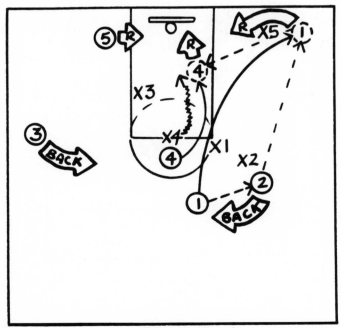

Figure 6-3
Give and Go Variation
Against 1-3-1 Zone
(Scoring opportunity for 0-4)

shoot from the corner or (3) pass to 0-4 for a short jumper or layup. All three possibilities should be attempted when you first set up in order to test the effectiveness of the defensive players. If they react as described, run all phases of this option over and over until the defense adjusts. When the defense begins to check these moves and consistently prevents the offense from scoring, move on to the other options covered in this section. Then, from time to time during the game, have the offensive players run these initial phases of the *Give and Go Variation* on the chance that the defense will fail to rotate properly, even though they may have made adjustments previously to block the option. You will find that the defense will tend to relax on these phases at times, and you can pick up a basket or two as a result.

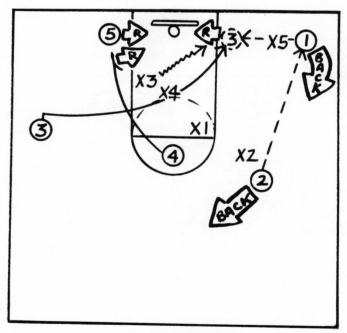

Figure 6-4
One to Three
Against 1-3-1 Zone

One to Three (Figure 4)

The *Three Man Across* option as a followup to the *Give and Go Variation* will not be so effective against zone defenses as it is against man-to-man defenses. If 0-2 should attempt to pass to 0-3 as 0-3 moves across the floor to the opposite low post position, the concentration of defensive men in the circle area would almost inevitably cause the pass to be deflected or intercepted. Therefore, you will want to move directly from the *Give and Go Variation* to the *One to Three* option. The setup will be similar to that of Figure 2; 0-1 has gone through to the corner and is being covered by X-5. As 0-2 passes the ball to 0-1, 0-3 moves over 0-4's screen and heads for the opposite low post spot (Figure 4). The backside man of the zone at the time (X-3) will be forced to pull over to cover 0-3, thus upsetting the balance of the 1-3-1 zone formation. This creates a one-on-one in the basket area and puts 0-3 in an excellent position to receive the pass from 0-1 for a turnaround jumper. X-4 cannot fall off and help because he would be leaving his responsibility to the middle.

Another possibility here includes a quick pass by 0-3 under the basket to 0-5 for a layup. Because of the overload situation, 0-5 will be wide open. The effectiveness of either of these moves will depend to a great extent on quickness, perfect timing, and 0-3's ability to immediately determine whether he or 0-5 will have the best chance of scoring.

Five Up (Figures 5 and 6)

This move is a valuable extension of the pattern against the zone defenses. Another followup of the *Give and Go Variation*, its success depends on the flexibility of the low post man in working with the outside guards to take advantage of the overload situation. It is especially useful when, as a result of defensive rotation, 0-1 is unable to get off his shot from the corner or 0-3 is blocked in his maneuvers in the *One to Three* option.

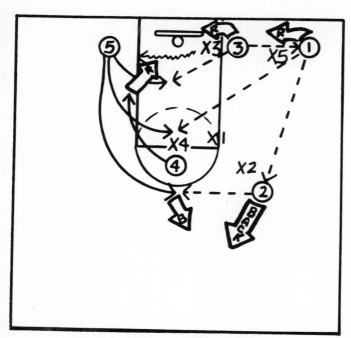

Figure 6-5
Five Up Against 1-3-1 Zone

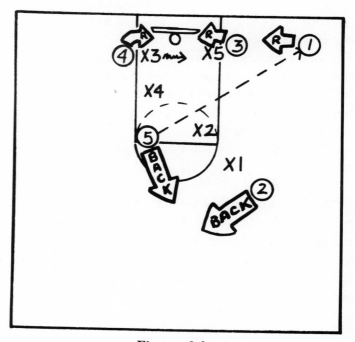

Figure 6-6
Five Up Against 1-3-1 Zone
(Pitch-off)

In Figure 5, 0-5 becomes aware that 0-1 and 0-3 cannot get a good shot away, so he immediately makes his move toward the free-throw area, looking for the pass for a quick jumper. He can either come up over 0-4, who is rolling to the basket, or he can make a sharp move in front of 0-4. This leaves X-4 in a difficult situation because his back is turned; he is attempting to cover 0-4 and at the same time trying to anticipate 0-5's move. X-5 cannot help because that would leave 0-1 free to shoot. X-3 has dropped off to play the backside of the zone, so he is unlikely to leave his area of responsibility to cover 0-5.

The combination of three factors makes this maneuver difficult to cover: (1) 0-5 is free to move to whatever section of the free-throw area he chooses; (2) his interchange with 0-4 is unexpected; and (3) 0-3 can make the pass directly to 0-5 or may hand off to 0-1 in the corner, who in turn can hit 0-5 or pass to 0-2, who then throws to 0-5. This flexibility will put the defense in a switch; it cannot react quickly enough to keep up with the ball.

Another move the offense can utilize if the other options have failed to produce a basket is a *Pitch-off* by 0-5 (Figure 6). If he is double-teamed or picked up by the defense after he has received the ball, he goes up for his jumper but pitches off instead to 0-1. 0-1 should be in the clear because the defense usually moves toward the ball side when the pass is made to 0-5. X-5 is busy checking 0-3, X-2 will drop off to the middle, and X-1 will probably be playing the outside man (0-2). X-3 has backside responsibility and has his hands full with 0-4, who has rolled to the basket. X-4 is at a great disadvantage because many of 0-5's moves will be behind him; in most cases he cannot turn and pick up 0-5 in time to hurt him.

Keep in mind that when 0-5 goes up for the jumper previous to the *Pitch-off*, the defense is expecting him to shoot and will turn toward the basket, looking for the rebound. Therefore, the pass to 0-1 is a surprise. Also, X-1 is shown playing his middle front responsibility area, which is at the front of the 1-3-1 zone.

If he leaves, and drops too far to the inside, then 0-2 can move over, receives the *Pitch-off* from 0-5, and have an open shot from the outside. Both the *Five Up* and the *Pitch-off* depend to a great extent on 0-5's ability to keep his head and to react to the circumstances in the most advantageous way.

Low Post Jumper or Pitch-off (Figures 7 and 8)

When using this option against a zone setup, your primary objective will be to develop a one-on-one for 0-5. This situation will be very difficult for the defense to cover and is more effective against the 1-3-1 zone than it is against other zones. As 0-1 passes to 0-3 and goes to the corner (Figure 7), X-2 will probably drop off 0-2 to cover 0-1, and X-1 will rotate over to guard 0-2. X-3 will move out to play 0-3 tight, but X-4 must remain close to 0-4 due to his top of the key position. Even though X-1 and X-2 are likely to slide toward the ball side as the ball is passed from 0-1 to 0-3, X-5 will ordinarily be left with one-on-one coverage of 0-5 when 0-5 receives the pass from 0-3. Any time the post man has this kind of situation, he should score or be fouled by X-5 while shooting the ball. X-2 is not likely to move all the way over to double-team, because that would leave 0-1 open in the corner.

If 0-3 sees that 0-5 has his one-on-one, he remains in his wing position while 0-5 goes for the basket. However, if he feels there is a possibility of 0-5 being double-teamed or checked, he goes through to the opposite low post (the overload situation) as shown in Figure 8. Then, if 0-5 is unable to get his shot away, he goes up for the jumper, but instead pitches off to 0-3 or to 0-1, depending on which man can get open and will have the best chance of scoring.

Attacking the 2-1-2 zone

When your team uses the M-C Offense against a 2-1-2 zone, your greatest advantage over the defensive players will be that you will force them to match up. The 2-1-2 is not designed as a

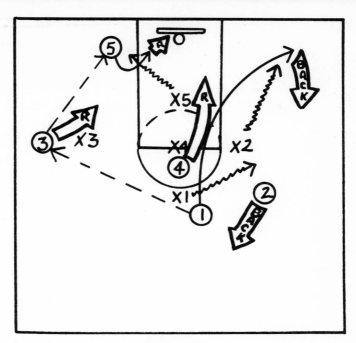

Figure 6-7
Low Post Jumper or Pitch-off
Against 1-3-1 Zone

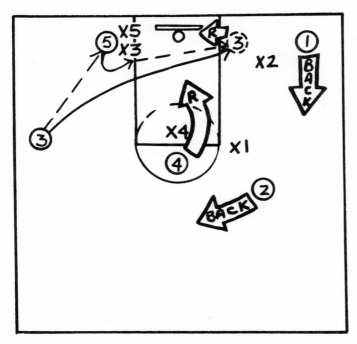

Figure 6-8
Low Post Jumper or Pitch-off
Against 1-3-1 Zone
(Pitch-off)

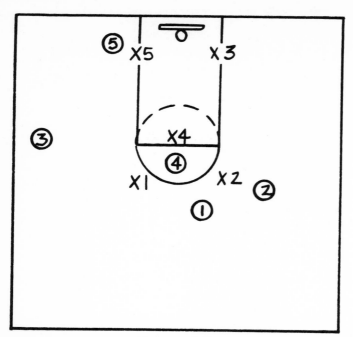

Figure 6-9
Basic Setup Against 2-1-2 Zone

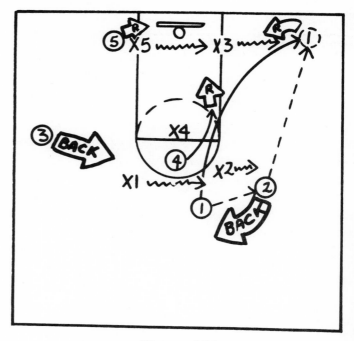

Figure 6-10
Give and Go Variation
Against 2-1-2 Zone

match-up defense; your opponents cannot match up and still be able to maintain zone responsibility. The offset at the front of the offensive setup will cause the defense to shift (overshift), and the opponents will be unable to make some of the rotation moves for which they are responsible.

The outside front defensive man (X-1) usually has top responsibility in the 2-1-2 formation (Figure 9). Normally he plays the ball outside and slides back to the free-throw line extended. However, when he moves over to cover 0-1, he still has the wing man (0-3) to worry about. He finds himself overextended with a two-on-one situation unless X-5 helps him, but X-5 has baseline responsibility and does not come out that far. X-2 ordinarily would help out, but he is held tight by 0-2, who will be handling the ball. This gives the offense a little more room on the inside in which to move the ball; and this inside movement is what the 2-1-2 zone is designed to prevent.

Give and Go Variation (Figure 10)

Start the pattern against the 2-1-2 as usual with the *Give and Go Variation* with the thought in mind of forcing the defense to match up at the beginning of the game (Figure 10). As 0-1 passes to 0-2 and goes through, the baseline man of the zone to the side of the ball (X-3) will have to cover him in the corner. X-3 is generally one of the strong rebounders, and this move will force him to defend an area away from the boards. X-5 will have to move over and help under the basket. If X-3 does not cover or does not move quickly enough, 0-1 will have a shot from the corner area when he receives the pass from 0-2. Also, if X-2 fails to move quickly on the initial pass, 0-2 will have an outside set shot.

One to Three (Figure 11)

As against the 1-3-1 zone, you will eliminate the possibility of a pass from 0-2 to 0-3 as 0-3 moves to the opposite low post position (*Three Man Across*). However, by sending 0-3 across

(Figure 11) you will force the offside baseline man (X-5) to match up; this will result in an overload. 0-1 can then pass to 0-3 who may either shoot or turn and hit 0-5 for a basket. X-5 will now have to play 0-3 tight, but X-4 may drop back to try to prevent the cut-off pass even though he still has responsibility on 0-4. X-1 and X-2 are unable to help because of their ballside commitment to 0-1 and 0-2. On this option it is difficult for the defense to rotate from the overload to the offside because X-4 would have to move all the way outside with 0-5.

Five Up (Figures 12 and 13)

If the defense adjusts to the preceding options, then turn to the *Five Up* move (Figure 12). 0-1 quickly passes the ball back to 0-2, who in turn takes a quick lateral bounce and then passes to 0-4 (who has moved back to the top of the key and pulls out

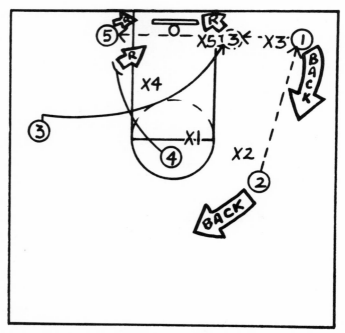

Figure 6-11
One to Three
Against 2-1-2 Zone

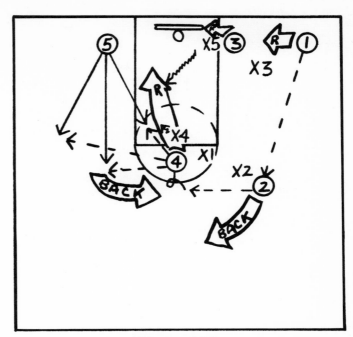

Figure 6-12
Five Up Against 2-1-2 Zone

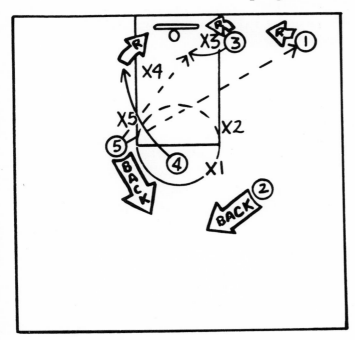

Figure 6-13
Five Up Against 2-1-2 Zone
(Pitch-off)

to receive the ball). 0-4 then hits 0-5, who is coming up on the offside away from the overload and is in position for a short jumper or has the option of maneuvering with the ball in the basket area. The key to this play lies in the ability of the players to move the ball quickly to the offside. An especially swift movement is necessary between 0-2 and 0-4, where care must be taken that X-1 does not pick up the pass. If the *Five Up* is executed properly, 0-5 will have good shooting position or a one-on-one on the offside; 0-1, 0-3, and 0-4 will move to the basket for the rebound.

While 0-5 pulls up with the ball or goes for the jumper, 0-4 and 0-3 should be moving as illustrated in Figure 13. 0-5 will be looking all the while to the inside players for a pitch-off or throw-off if he feels that he will not have a good shot. Since the defensive players will have turned their backs to 0-5, expecting a shot from him, his pitch-off to 0-3 or 0-1 (or possibly to 0-4 if the zone fails to rotate properly) will be a surprise, and the receiver will be in good position to get off a shot before the defense has time to react.

Low Post Jumper or Pitch-off (Figure 14)

Here is another option that will force the 2-1-2 zone defense to match up. When 0-1 passes to 0-3 and goes through, the backside defensive men (X-3 and X-5) may rotate as shown in Figure 14. When 0-1 makes his move to the corner, the rotation of X-1 and X-2 on 0-1 and 0-2 will throw the defense into a 3-2 zone. When 0-3 passes the ball to 0-5, 0-5 will have a one-on-one with X-3 and should be able to score from this position or be fouled in the act of shooting. He also has the possibility of making a quick pitch-off. Since the offense has made the zone shift from its normal 2-1-2 coverage to a 3-2 coverage, the defense is at a disadvantage because the rotation rules on the two zones are different. This can result in confusion among the defensive players.

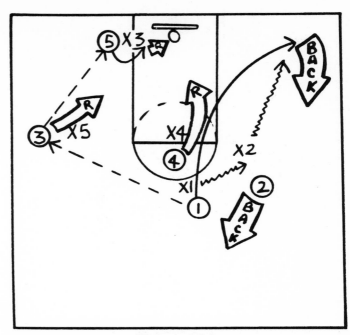

Figure 6-14
Low Post Jumper or Pitch-off
Against 2-1-2 Zone

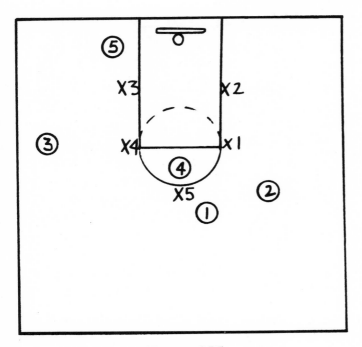

Figure 6-15
Basic Setup Against 1-2-2 Zone

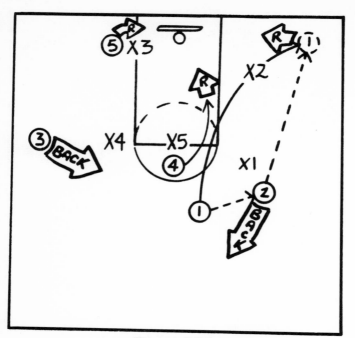

Figure 6-16
Give and Go Variation
Against 1-2-2 Zone

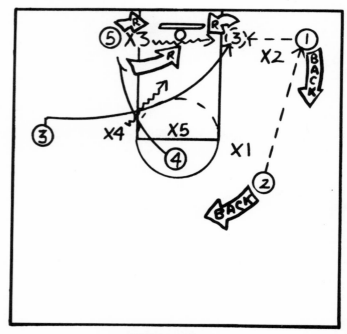

Figure 6-17
One to Three
Against 1-2-2 Zone

Attacking the 1-2-2 zone

The 1-2-2 zone is strong on the inside and is used to force the offensive players to make their moves on the outside. It has a tendency to give you the good outside shot (depending on the individual coach) but keeps the inside closed up in order to prevent short passes from being made to the inside offensive players. Figure 15 shows the basic offensive setup against the 1-2-2 zone.

Give and Go Variation (Figure 16)

In Figure 16 you can see that the *Give and Go Variation* causes the defense to shift somewhat, but not enough to be penetrated. If the baseline man (X-2) does not come all the way out, encourage 0-1 to shoot, and form the rebounding cup with 0-3, 0-4, and 0-5. Against the 1-2-2 the outside guards will force a quick matchup with X-1 and X-2.

One to Three (Figure 17)

As the wing man (0-3) goes across (Figure 17), the defense adjusts even more to a matchup, yet they are still strong on the inside. When he moves across to the low post position, 0-3 should set up at an angle so that the pass from 0-1 need not be a lob pass over the defense. This option forces the offside baseline man (X-3) to pick up 0-3, giving 0-3 a quick one-on-one as he goes for the basket. The defense will usually set up tight and force the offense; in this situation 0-3 is often double-teamed. If so, he can pass the ball back to 0-1 for an outside corner shot.

Five Up (Figure 18)

Although the *One to Three* option is generally crowded by the defense, it does make the opponent adjust or match up and leaves the way open for the *Five Up*. You can see in Figure 18

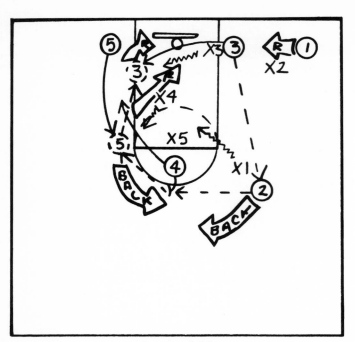

Figure 6-18
Five Up
Against 1-2-2 Zone

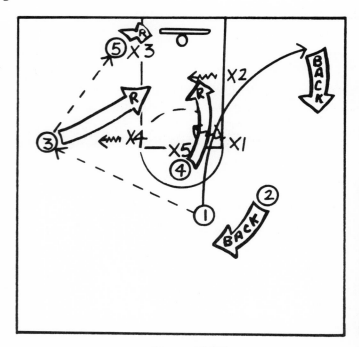

Figure 6-19
Low Post Jumper or Pitch-off
Against 1-2-2 Zone

how tough this move will be to cover against a 1-2-2 zone. It leaves the offside baseline area open for 0-3, who will make a quick move back to the inside, beating the defense.

The pass is made from 0-3 to 0-2. 0-2 then either passes to 0-4 or sends a cross-court bounce pass to 0-5, who is moving up toward the free-throw line extended. 0-3 knows that this option on the offside is coming up, so he beats the defense (X-3) to his position for a one-on-one. Then 0-4 or 0-5, depending on who has received the ball from 0-2, flips the ball back to 0-3, who is now open and in good position for a short jumper. X-4 has had to pull outside to cover 0-5, leaving the basket area open. X-3 adjusts to the middle of the lane, X-1 has dropped off toward the ball side, and X-5 still has middle free-throw lane responsibility on 0-4.

Low Post Jumper or Pitch-off (Figure 19)

This option (Figure 19) is very strong, especially against the 1-2-2. The zone generally does not like to come very far out on the wing man (0-3) and will give him that outside shot to help protect the inside. Put your best shooter on the 3 spot against this type of zone and tell him to shoot the ball when he receives it from 0-1 instead of passing to 0-5. If the defense does not pick him up, let him continue to shoot. This will be a good, sound offensive shot because 0-3 has time to set, being under control and having good balance. Most coaches will tell X-4 to cheat out a little but will not move him all the way out until 0-3 makes from one to three baskets. Then X-4 has to play him tight, so 0-3 will pass off to 0-5 for the *Back Door or Pitch-out.*

Back Door or Pitch-out (Figure 20)

The *Back Door* option is the strongest option of the M-C attack against a 1-2-2 zone that plays you real tough on the inside. In Figure 20, 0-5 receives the pass from 0-3. If he thinks he can beat his man (X-3), he reverses and uses the back-door

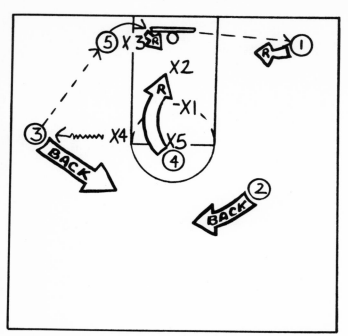

Figure 6-20
Back Door or Pitch-out
Against 1-2-2 Zone

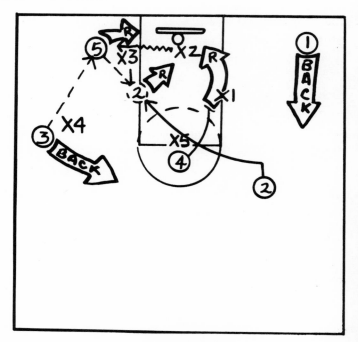

Figure 6-21
Two Man Through
Against 1-2-2 Zone

shot. If he does not have a shot after his reverse (because X-2 cheats over for a double-team with X-3), he will bounce pass or pitch out to 0-1, who is in the corner and who should be open. This move is difficult for the defense to cover because the defense has been forced to match up, and the offside man of the zone (X-2) must attempt to cover 0-1 and try to check 0-5 at the same time. If he does not check, 0-5 shoots; if he does check, 0-5 bounces to 0-1 for the basket. This option also eliminates excessive passing and ball handling, thus strengthening the offensive attack because the players have fewer chances of losing the ball on a turnover.

Two Man Through (Figure 21)

The *Two Man Through,* the final option against the 1-2-2 zone, is used primarily when 0-5 is consistently double-teamed by X-3 and X-2. In Figure 21, 0-1 has passed to 0-3 and is in the corner. X-4 has pulled out to stop 0-3's outside shot, so 0-3 passes to 0-5. X-3 is playing 0-5 tight, and the offside baseline man (X-2) moves over to help X-3 with the double-team. 0-5 cannot make an overhead pass to 0-1 because X-1 is splitting the difference between 0-1 and 0-2, inviting a very dangerous pass.

In this situation, you have 0-2 delay for the sure double-team and then come through to the ball over 0-4's screen. He receives the pass from 0-5 and either goes in for a layup or pulls up for a short jumper. X-4 is unable to drop off and help because he has 0-3 to cover in case of a quick pass back to 0-3 from 0-5. X-1 will not move with 0-2 because of his zone area, so 0-2 should be able to pick up a basket. The defense is in close, but this quick pass from 0-5 to 0-2 can be made, and the defense cannot adjust quickly enough to stop it. Too, experience has shown that 0-2 will be fouled often on this option. 0-1 will move back outside for balance, and 0-3, 0-4, and 0-5 are set for the rebound.

Attacking the 2-3 zone

The 2-3 zone is not so popular as the 1-3-1, the 2-1-2, or the 1-2-2, but it is used at times to make the inside especially strong in order to stop the big man from getting the ball or to keep him off the boards. The 2-3 will sometimes shift into a 2-1-2, depending on where the big man plays. Most offensive teams will keep their big man low and inside; as a result the middle man on the 2-3 setup is low. Double-blocking the big man off the boards is the greatest advantage for the defense using the 2-3 zone, but you will find that offensive shooting areas are more easily obtained than they are against other zones.

Figure 22 illustrates the basic 2-3 zone defensive setup. Since most high school teams use two guards with their offensive pattern, this defense attempts to force the offensive players to match up and will be effective against teams who do not have much movement on offense. However, because the primary objective of any offense is to force the defense to match up (not vice versa) you will have the defense at a disadvantage if you can force them to match up with the offensive players. This matchup is what the following options will accomplish.

Give and Go Variation (Figure 23)

In Figure 23, the *Give and Go Variation* has already forced the defense to match up. The middle man (X-5) is still covering close on the inside, but the other defensive men have had to rotate (more than likely) from their normal defensive areas. The *Give and Go* will score here if X-5 does not drop off and pick up 0-1 as he goes through. X-5 has moved up and covered 0-4, and X-3 has dropped off to the backside, helping in the lane. X-1 will take the outside *Give and Go* man (0-1) when he gets to his area. 0-1 can receive the pass from 0-2 and will have a jumper if X-1 does not pick him up quickly enough.

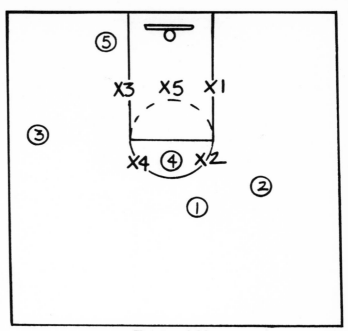

Figure 6-22
Basic Setup
Against 2-3 Zone

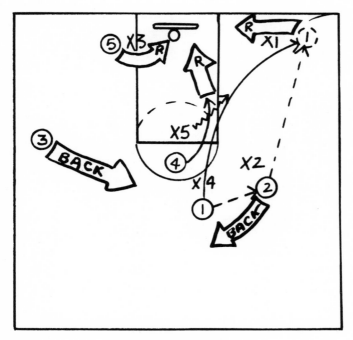

Figure 6-23
Give and Go Variation
Against 2-3 Zone

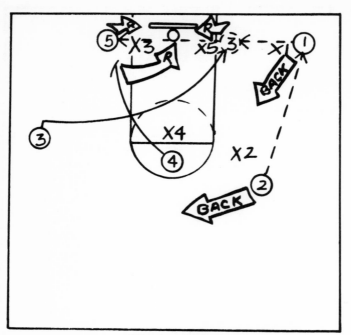

Figure 6-24
One to Three
Against 2-3 Zone

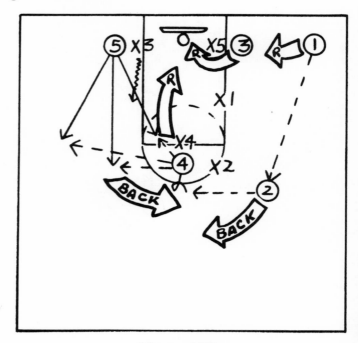

Figure 6-25
Five Up
Against 2-3 Zone

One to Three (Figure 24)

In Figure 24 you cause the defense to lose their potential double coverage on 0-5 by overloading. X-5 has to leave his responsibility area and move over to cover 0-3, who has come across. This leaves X-3 with single coverage on the big man (0-5). X-4 has dropped off from the outside, picking up 0-4 (who most probably is taller and stronger than X-4), and X-1 is still covering 0-1 in the corner. Again the defense is in a matchup. 0-3, after receiving the quick pass from 0-1, turns and throws a high lob pass to 0-5 for a basket. The defense still has good baseline coverage but has lost the double-team on the offensive big man, and the rebounding situation is more evenly balanced. Thus you have nullified the two strong points of the 2-3 zone defense.

Five Up (Figure 25)

Here is an alternative method in which to get the ball to 0-5 and take advantage of the fact that the *One to Three* option has thrown the defense into a matchup on the overload. In Figure 25, X-1 and X-5 loosen up a little as the ball is passed back from 0-1 to 0-2. However, they will not overextend themselves because they are still to the ball side. As 0-2 receives the ball, X-2 will continue to play him tight; X-4 must play 0-4 tight because of the position of the ball, and X-5 has middle baseline responsibility. 0-4 pulls out quickly to receive the pass from 0-2, and before the zone can shift 0-5 moves up to get the pass from 0-4. 0-5 will now have a one-on-one with X-3 and can take a jumper or use his own individual moves to maneuver for a basket. The defense will be unable to shift quickly enough to keep up with the offensive men. If X-2 is ineffective as a cut-off pass man, the offside area will be left vulnerable.

Two Man Through (Figure 26)

The defense has now shifted back into the original 2-3 zone on this option with the exception of X-3, who has pulled out to cover 0-5. The inside balance is just about like it was. In Figure 26, with the ball on the offside (0-5 has it), the zone has moved toward the ball; X-2 is playing the offside free-throw line area, and X-5 has dropped off to help out on the inside lane. X-1 has also moved back toward the lane to help inside. X-4 still has man-to-man coverage on 0-4.

You would think that the defense has no weakness on the inside. However, X-2 is not aware of 0-2's position, other than his playing on the outside. As soon as X-2 moves toward the ball to help out, 0-2 makes his move to the basket. X-2 will be unable to pick up 0-2 because he has his back to him. X-1 cannot pick him up quickly enough; if he does, he is leaving the passing lane open to 0-1 and 0-3. X-4 cannot sink off and help on the cutter because it will leave 0-4 open at the circle. X-3 can get there, but not quickly enough, and usually fouls 0-2. This option results in a number of free throws for 0-2 or should give him a field goal.

Low Post Jumper or Pitch-off (Figure 27)

The setup on offense in Figure 27 causes the 2-3 zone to lose its effectiveness because the middle man must come high to play 0-4, and the defense is shifted into a 2-1-2 zone. The rotation of the 2-3 zone will lose its rules against this type of setup. Then, after the first pass is made from 0-1 to 0-3, the defense matches up into a 3-2 zone. 0-3 passes the ball to 0-5, who has a one-on-one situation with X-3. X-1 and X-2 are helping out toward the ball side but cannot cheat too much. If X-3 is over-playing 0-5, 0-5 may pull out a little to get the ball and then maneuver X-3 in and around the baseline area with his offensive moves, going for a basket or being fouled in the act of shooting. Or, 0-5 always has the alternative of pitching off if another man is open and has a better chance to score.

The box-and-1 zone

The Box-and-1 zone defense is not used so much as it was in years past. It was designed to stop a particular offensive ball

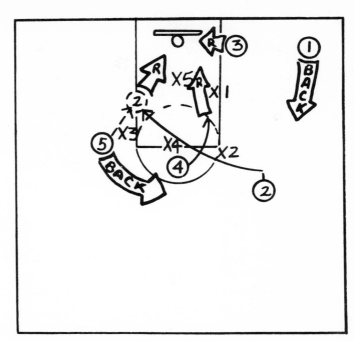

Figure 6-26
Two Man Through
Against 2-3 Zone

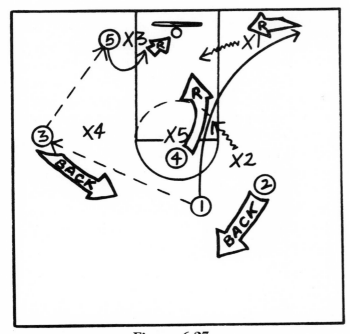

Figure 6-27
Low Post Jumper or Pitch-off
Against 2-3 Zone

player or to put more than usual pressure on him. It has lost its effectiveness, since high school players have become such prolific shooters. Since the M-C Offense has so many options and is not geared around one player, the Box-and-1 zone defense would be completely ineffective against it.

Summary

This chapter has provided convincing evidence of the value of the Multiple-Continuous Offense against four of the more common zone defenses. As a rule, the most effective options against zone defenses will be the *Give and Go Variation, One to Three, Five Up,* and *Low Post Jumper or Pitch-off.* In addition, the *Two Man Through* is of value against two zones, and the *Back Door or Pitch-out* will be extremely helpful against the 1-2-2 zone. You may find that some of the other options will work equally well against the zone setup of a given opponent, especially if the overall defensive ability of his players is weak.

Following is an abbreviated checklist of the most effective options against each of the zone defenses that are covered in this chapter with notations of the probable shooter or shooters from each option. Refer to it as you formulate your game plans so that you will be certain to include the most suitable options against the specific zone defense you will be faced with.

Note: 0-4 is listed as possible shooter only twice. There are times, as he rolls to the basket on the various options, that he will be open. If so, he can receive a quick pass for a layup or short jumper.

Against a 1-3-1 Zone

Give and Go Variation (Shooters: 0-1, 0-2, or 0-4)
One to Three (Shooters: 0-3 or 0-5)
Five Up (Shooters: 0-5, 0-1, or 0-2)
Low Post Jumper or *Pitch-off* (Shooters: 0-5, 0-3, or 0-1)

Against a 2-1-2 Zone

Give and Go Variation (Shooters: 0-1 or 0-2)
One to Three (Shooters: 0-3 or 0-5)
Five Up (Shooters: 0-5, 0-3, 0-1, or possibly 0-4)
Low Post Jumper or *Pitch-off* (Shooter: 0-5 or pitch-off)

Against a 1-2-2 Zone

Give and Go Variation (Shooter: 0-1)
One to Three (Shooters: 0-3 or 0-1)
Five Up (Shooter: 0-3)
Low Post Jumper or *Pitch-off* (Shooters: 0-3 or 0-5)
Back Door or *Pitch-out* (Shooters: 0-5 or 0-1)
Two Man Through (Shooter: 0-2)

Against a 2-3 Zone

Give and Go Variation (Shooter: 0-1)
One to Three (Shooter: 0-5)
Five Up (Shooter: 0-5)
Two Man Through (Shooter: 0-2)
Low Post Jumper or *Pitch-off* (Shooter: 0-5 or pitch-off)

7

Combating Man-to-Man Defenses with the M-C Offense

You have seen in Chapter 6 how effective the Multiple-Continuous Offense can be against zone defenses. Now it is time to take a look at how it will work against man-to-man defenses. This chapter will cover the use of this offense against the basic man-to-man defense and three of its variations: the tight (overplaying) man-to-man, the sinking man-to-man, and the switching man-to-man. The options to use, how to run them for maximum effectiveness, and the probable reaction of the defensive players to these options will be discussed in connection with these four types of man-to-man defense.

Attacking the basic man-to-man

The basic man-to-man is the easiest type of defense to play against when using the Multiple-Continuous Offense, and you will find that this offense will be most effective against it insofar as the use of all the options of the pattern and the freedom of continuity allowed the offensive players in moving from one option to another are concerned. The basic man-to-man will not apply the additional pressure that is found in the man-to-man variations—the tight, sinking, or switching man-to-man defenses.

When encountering the team that employs the basic man-to-man defense, the offense may feel free to run all the pattern options exactly as they are outlined in Chapters 4 and 5 without any adjustments. However, if the defensive players should occasionally try a switch or use any other maneuver typical of a man-to-man variation, the offensive men will have no difficulty in operating if they are familiar with the adjustments which must be made against the other forms of man-to-man defense discussed in this chapter. For example, if the defense finds that it is being hurt and goes to a combination defensive attack, the offensive players can quickly make a few minor adjustments and continue their options.

The following options, which are discussed in detail in Chapters 4 and 5, may all be used with confidence against the basic man-to-man defense: *Give and Go Variation, Three Man Across, One to Three, Five Up, Basic Give and Go, Outside Reverse, Big Man—Little Man Switch, Inside Give and Go, Low Post Jumper or Pitch-off, Back Door or Pitch-out,* and *Two Man Through.*

Attacking the tight (overplaying) man-to-man

This type of defense is designed primarily for the purpose of preventing the pattern-minded offensive team from running its pattern and causing it to lose part of its continuity. It also attempts to push or force the man with the ball by not giving him as much of an opportunity to operate on offense with the ball as other defenses do. In attacking a team playing this type of defense, the team using the M-C Offense knows that it will need to make some adjustments, but not so many that it will

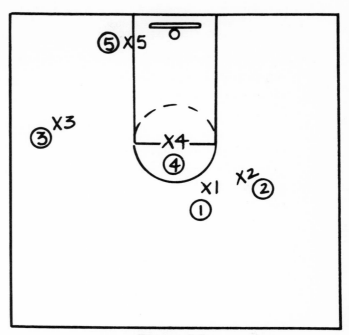

Figure 7-1
Basic Give and Go Against Tight
(Overplaying) Man-to-Man

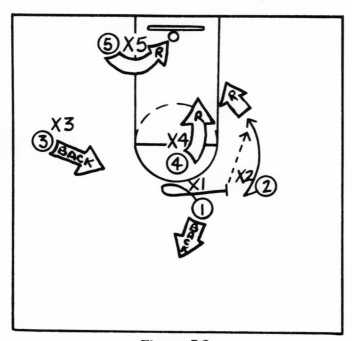

Figure 7-2
Basic Give and Go Against Tight
(Overplaying) Man-to-Man

have to get completely away from its pattern. The options that have proved successful against the tight (overplaying) man-to-man defense are as follows:

Basic Give and Go (Figures 1 and 2)

This option finds X-1 cheating or overplaying 0-1, the ball man, to his right and inviting him to go left (Figure 1); X-2 is overplaying 0-2 in an attempt to cut off the pass from 0-1. The defensive positions of X-3, X-4, and X-5 are normal man-to-man positions. This leaves the offense with a two-on-two situation for 0-1 and 0-2; thus these outside guards will have room to maneuver. If X-1 is overplaying 0-1 to the extreme and is forcing him left, 0-1 (in Figure 2) starts the option by driving to his left and reversing at the top of the key, using 0-4 as a screener. He now has hung X-1 up enough that he can take the ball on the dribble with his right hand to the other outside guard to set up the option. X-2 is overextended to prevent the pass from 0-1 to 0-2 and is in perfect position for the *Give and Go* to work. As 0-1 starts looking for 0-2's move, 0-2 fakes his left foot and body with a quick jab step and then goes backside of X-2 toward the basket. Now X-1 is head up with 0-1, and X-2 is overextended and cannot recover in time to stop 0-2, who has gone toward the basket and is looking for the pass. As soon as 0-1 sees that 0-2 has beat his man, he pulls up with the ball and uses the right-hand jumper pass to 0-2, who is free for the quick jumper or possibly a layup. If this option is executed properly, several baskets can be picked up, primarily because of the overplaying position of the defensive players. The importance of timing should be stressed to your outside guards on this option.

Three Man Across (Figures 3 and 4)

Using this option and working it effectively depends on the ability of the outside guard (0-2) to get free so that the option can be started. In Figure 3, X-2 is shown overplaying and tight

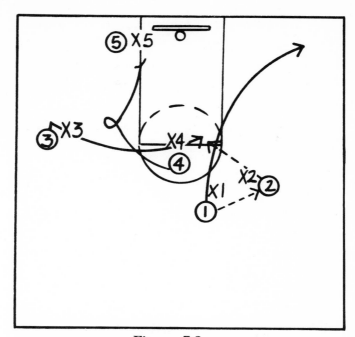

Figure 7-3
Three Man Across Against Tight
(Overplaying) Man-to-Man

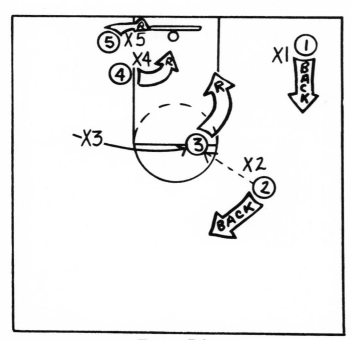

Figure 7-4
Three Man Across Against Tight
(Overplaying) Man-to-Man

on 0-2. 0-2 fakes to the basket and loosens out a little in order to receive the pass from 0-1. After 0-1 has made the pass, he continues to the corner and sets up, taking X-1 with him. 0-4, the top post man, starts his move away from the ball as soon as 0-2 receives the ball from 0-1. He sets a hesitating screen on X-3 as he continues to the basket toward low post. 0-3 has faked the baseline with his left foot (quick jab step) and comes sharply off the screen with a long step with his right foot. The momentary screen on X-3 allows the offensive wing man to get free; as he goes across he is looking for the pass from the outside guard (0-2). 0-2 makes the left-hand bounce pass or an over-the-head pass to 0-3, who is now open in the free-throw line area. 0-3 receives the pass and takes his jumper or has the option for the layup; his shot will depend on how quickly the defense recovers. In Figure 4, the positions of the offensive and defensive players are given to allow the coach to see the actual positions of the players as the option is completed. X-3 is shown parallel to 0-3; this will be his normal position when 0-4 has set the screen effectively. Notice that the move that makes this option successful against the tight man-to-man actually occurs away from the pass. As you have seen, no adjustment to the basic option has been necessary to combat this particular defensive attack.

Low Post Jumper or Pitch-off (Figures 5 and 6)

The success of this option against the tight man-to-man is dependent on the wing man (0-3). In Figure 5, the defense is shown overplaying 0-1, 0-2, 0-3, and 0-5. However, X-1 has given 0-1 room to go to his left without too much pressure. The option is started by 0-1 dribbling the ball with his left hand toward the wing man. Since 0-3 is being overplayed, he (0-3) makes a fake to the outside with his left foot, then rocks back with his right foot and receives the pass from 0-1; 0-1 goes on through to the corner. Because X-5 is overplaying 0-5 and discouraging the pass from 0-3, 0-5 leaves his low post spot, makes

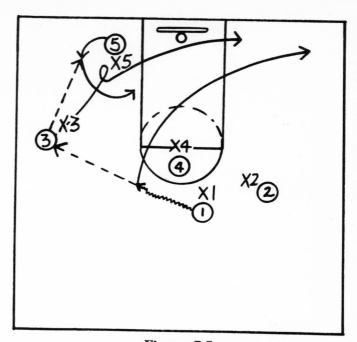

Figure 7-5
Low Post Jumper or Pitch-off
Against Tight (Overplaying) Man-to-Man

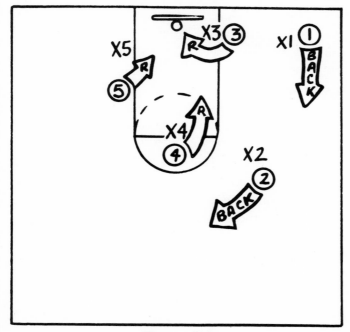

Figure 7-6
Low Post Jumper or Pitch-off
Against Tight (Overplaying) Man-to-Man

a quick move to the ball, and can now safely receive the pass from 0-3. 0-3 then starts his move to X-5 for the screen, planting his right foot to the inside of X-5's left foot. He sets the screen, 0-5 comes over the screen with the ball, and 0-3 continues to the basket and sets up in the opposite low post position. 0-5 has the advantage on X-5, who must recover if he hopes to keep 0-5 from scoring.

Figure 6 shows the floor position of the defensive players using the tight (overplaying) man-to-man defense after their reactions to the moves of the option. The offensive balance is good, and another option can be initiated if this option is checked. Again, this type of defense has not forced the offense to make any major adjustments in the option. The *Low Post Jumper* can be a very important option because the big man at the low post position ends up with the definite advantage, and this is what all coaches strive and work for. Obviously, the ability of the low post man to get open and free from his defensive man is important to the success of this option. It is designed for the low post man who does not have a lot of quickness and reaction time. So, he finds that if he will pull out, he can receive the pass from 0-3. On the other hand, a coach who has a low post man with the ability to get free automatically to receive the pass by outmaneuvering his defensive man is quick to see the one-on-one potential of the low post position in this option.

Two Man Through (Figures 7, 8, 9, and 10)

If for any reason the *Low Post Jumper* does not work, the offensive players know immediately that the *Two Man Through* will be the next option to use. In Figure 6 you saw how the situation stands as 0-5 goes for the jumper. If 0-2, the outside guard, sees that 0-5 does not have the basket from his option, he starts his move to the right of the high post man (0-4) and comes back over to the left of the screen set by 0-4 (Figure 7). X-2 is hung up by 0-4's screen and cannot recover quickly enough for good defensive position. 0-2, after moving off the

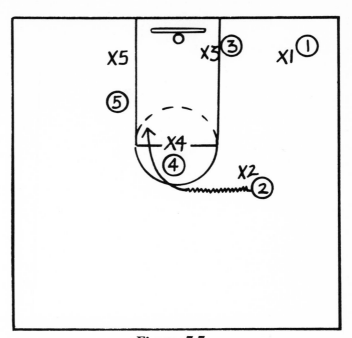

Figure 7-7
Two Man Through Against Tight
(Overplaying) Man-to-Man

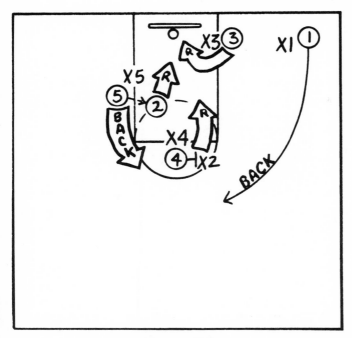

Figure 7-8
Two Man Through Against Tight
(Overplaying) Man-to-Man

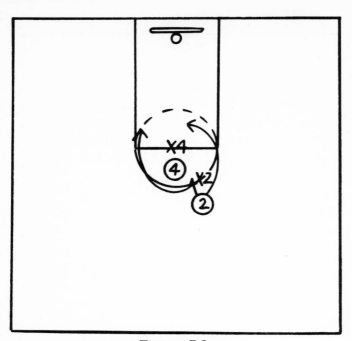

Figure 7-9
Two Man Through
Fake and Step Back Move

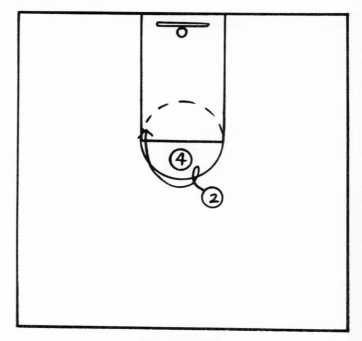

Figure 7-10
Two Man Through
Reverse Off Screen

screen, immediately starts looking for the pass from 0-5. 0-5 will be anticipating this option and is quick to see the opening for 0-2. 0-5 makes the pass (right-hand bounce pass, quick chest pass, or jumper pass) to 0-2, who will at times be able to penetrate for the layup or be fouled, or has the quick jumper inside the free-throw line.

Figure 8 illustrates the position of the defense and offense after 0-2 goes through. 0-2 will be free just below the free-throw line, so 0-5 can make the pass as 0-2 comes through anywhere from 0-4's screen to the bottom of the circle. X-2's position is shown as he has been caught by 0-4's screen; X-3 will still be on the inside covering 0-3, and X-1 is in the corner area with 0-1. The rebounding position on this option is strong for the offense because it will have 0-5, 0-3, and 0-4 on the inside to go to the boards; 0-1 will rotate back to the outside for defensive purposes. Another advantage of this option against the tight man-to-man is that the option is started by an offensive player who is away from the ball. This nullifies any advantage the defense might have in overplaying or cutting off a pass. Also, the offensive player (0-2) can put extra pressure on his defensive man because he is going for the basket; X-2 recognizes his responsibility of cutting off the pass to 0-2 but is frustrated in his attempt by 0-4's screen. You might assume automatically that, because of the proximity of defensive men in the area, 0-2 will not have much room in which to work; however, he will nearly always be able to get through to the ball. In the event he should be covered inside by a quick switch, he knows that someone has to be open as a result and that 0-5 can quickly adjust and pass to the open man.

0-2's ability to make this option work depends on how well he fakes X-2 and comes off the screen set by 0-4. In Figure 9, 0-2 has the option of going over the screen fronting the ball, or he can cut behind 0-4 as 0-4 moves to the basket. The technique of going over the screen fronting the ball is recommended for 0-2 in this case because (1) it gives him a good picture of the offensive and defensive players' positions; (2) he will be able to see the ball at all times; and (3) he knows that he has help from 0-4 with the advantage of the screen. The fake and step-back (rocker step) shown in Figure 9 is preferred over the reverse move (Figure 10). By using the fake and step-back method 0-2 will have the opportunity to go either way, to the right or to the left on 0-4's move. If he should use the reverse technique on the screen, he would have his back to the ball momentarily. In the fake and step-back technique, 0-2 fakes X-2 with his move to the right of 0-4, landing on his right foot. He recovers and shifts back to the weight of his left foot, switching his momentum to the left side as he begins his move to the basket. This option requires coordination and agility from 0-2 and good timing on the part of both 0-2 and 0-4.

0-2 will be able to pick up some crucial baskets with the *Two Man Through*. This move could be included in your game plan as the option to use to obtain the "clutch" basket in the situation where you have the ball with ten seconds left on the clock. It is ideal for such a situation because (1) the shot will be taken close in, with excellent rebounding positioning on the part of the offense, and (2) the opponent will tend to foul 0-2 frequently on this option—thus the possibility of free throws for the offense may be anticipated.

Attacking the sinking man-to-man

The primary goal of the team using the sinking man-to-man defense is to keep the offense away from the inside. It concentrates its efforts on preventing drives, discouraging layups, and stopping the inside big man. This necessarily leaves the outside game more open, but most coaches prefer to give the offensive team the outside areas rather than the inside since the shooting percentages of the outside players will usually be lower than those of the forwards and post man. Against this defense, then, either the coach must come up with a good, balanced attack or have complete confidence in his inside attack and feel that it is strong enough to win, regardless of what the defense does. In the latter instance an extra-strong inside attack may be successful against the sinking man-to-man in some cases, but usually is not consistently so from game to game. Too, many sinking man-to-man defenses produce the effect of a partial zone and will be tough to handle for offensive teams which have little or no continuity of movement.

The Multiple-Continuous Offense can cause the sinking man-to-man to lose much of its effectiveness, because the offensive players will be moving and screening, forcing more honest coverage from the defense. The pattern continuity and elements of surprise in this offense will prove their usefulness and will help offset any moves the defense may make. The players will know that if the Inside Attack is checked to a degree, they can turn to the Outside Attack. Thus the coach can combine the two attacks in the game plan in such a way that the defense will be forced to react both to outside and inside moves and will have to make more adjustments on defense than usual. It is true that the offense will need to vary some of the options somewhat when combating the sinking man-to-man, but not to such an extent that the basic pattern must be changed. You will find that this defense creates fewer problems for the Multiple-Continuous Offense than any other type of man-to-man (other than the basic man-to-man) and that most of the options will be effective against it.

Give and Go Variation (Figures 11 and 12)

The attack against the sinking man-to-man defense begins with the *Give and Go Variation* (Figure 11). 0-1 passes the ball to 0-2 and starts his move toward the left. He then comes back toward the ball, dragging X-1 off the screen set by 0-4, and makes his cut to the basket. 0-1 is now free momentarily to receive the ball from 0-2, who can either use a quick over-the-head jumper pass or a quick left-handed bounce pass. The defensive positions of X-1 and X-2 on this option will not vary

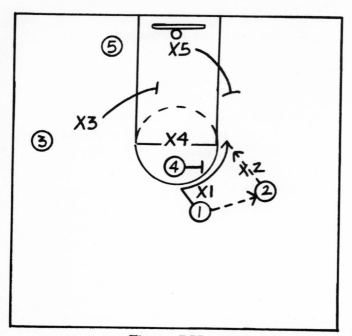

Figure 7-11
Give and Go Variation
Against Sinking Man-to-Man

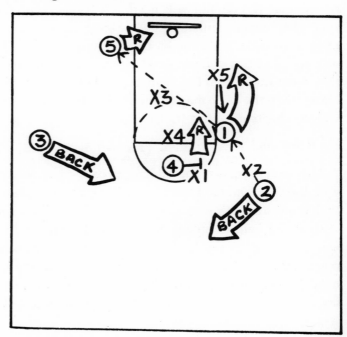

Figure 7-12
Give and Go Variation
Against Sinking Man-to-Man

too much from basic man-to-man coverage because they both have ball man responsibility. However, X-5 will probably sink off to the middle lane, while X-3 will drop off 0-3 to help toward the ball. X-4, on the other hand, must maintain his position on the top post man.

The danger of the sinking man-to-man on this option lies in the possibility of the defense cutting off the driver, 0-1. However, by doing this the defense will leave the inside vulnerable. If X-5 pulls out to cover 0-1 and X-3 slides further than he should toward the ball, the low post man (0-5) will be free. Thus if 0-1 is checked by X-5, he can send a quick bounce pass to 0-5 for the basket (Figure 12). If X-3 does drop off or rotate far enough to halfway check 0-5, 0-5 still has the advantage of the one-on-one inside. If the defense should play for the charging violation from the offensive guard (0-1) with X-5 playing position and then moving sharply in front of 0-1, attempting to force 0-1 to foul him, the quick pull up by 0-1 is used and he will be free to take a jumper or has the option of the bounce pass to 0-5. This technique of the defense will be used by the sinking man-to-man to discourage the outside guard from going on in for the layup, but 0-1 can make the adjustment quickly and the offense should still be able to score.

Three Man Across (Figures 13 and 14)

In Figure 13, the *Three Man Across* option is begun when 0-1 passes to 0-2 and goes through to set up in the corner and 0-4 starts his move away from the ball to set a hesitating screen for 0-3. Figure 14 shows the position of the sinking man-to-man defense after these two moves have been initiated. X-3 is sinking off 0-3 toward the ball man (0-2) and is in ideal position to be screened by 0-4, the high post man. X-4 must play 0-4 honest because he is moving toward the basket, but X-5 is covering the middle lane area, having dropped off 0-5 to play toward the ball area. X-1 has dropped away from 0-1 in the corner area to help out, and X-2 is playing the outside guard

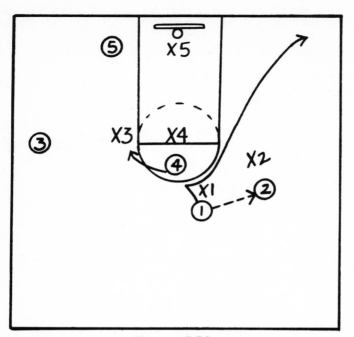

Figure 7-13
Three Man Across
Against Sinking Man-to-Man

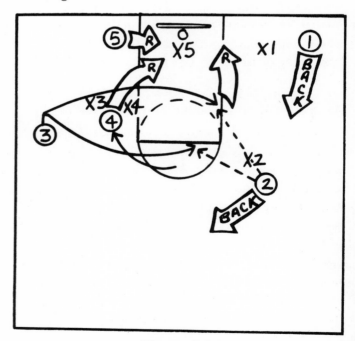

Figure 7-14
Three Man Across
Against Sinking Man-to-Man

in a normal defensive position because he has strict ball responsibility. In this situation X-3 is at a disadvantage because he
knows if he gets through the screen set by 0-4 that 0-3 will be
quick to see this and will use the back-door move off the screen.
If he plays the waiting game to check the screen and then gets
through, 0-3 will have already beat him over the top and will
have time to receive the ball around the free-throw line for the
quick jumper. X-1's position is not close enough to sink or drop
off to help, and X-2 cannot pick up 0-3 because he is playing
the ball man, 0-2. X-5's position under the basket will not allow
him to check 0-3 because of the distance involved; if he
attempts it, 0-3 will pitch off to 0-5, who would be left free
under the basket.

The *Three Man Across* option is very effective against the
sinking or helping man-to-man defense and definitely gives the
offensive team the opportunity of taking advantage of the three
phases of pattern movement: (1) 0-1's move to the corner to
the ball side, (2) 0-4's screen away from the ball, and (3) 0-3's
fake to the baseline and move to the ball either over the screen
or backdoor off the screen set by 0-4.

Outside Reverse (Figures 15 and 16)

The *Outside Reverse* is started by 0-2 clearing and going
through. Then 0-1 dribbles the ball with his left hand to 0-4's
right foot, and 0-4 sets the screen on X-1 as 0-1 begins his
reverse (Figure 15). 0-1 reverses back over the screen for the
quick jumper at the top of the doll's head or has the option to
maneuver in closer to the basket for his jumper. 0-1's advantage
on this option is evidenced by Figure 16. X-1 is ineffective
because he is unable to recover quickly enough to cover 0-1's
jumper. X-4 cannot help on the ball because he must maintain
coverage of 0-4. X-5 cannot cover the shooter because he is too
far out and 0-1's position does not fall under X-5's defensive
responsibility. X-2 cannot pick up 0-1 because 0-2 has made his
move to the basket on the ball side, and X-2 must cover him

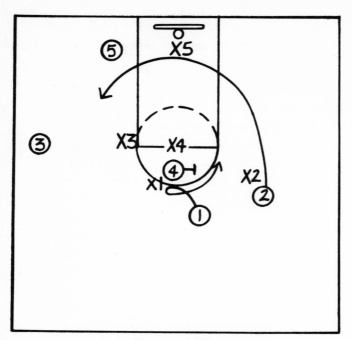

Figure 7-15
Outside Reverse
Against Sinking Man-to-Man

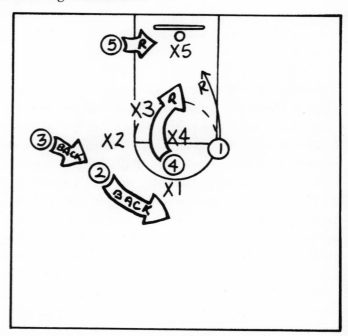

Figure 7-16
Outside Reverse
Against Sinking Man-to-Man

for the *Give and Go* possibility; then after 0-2 goes through, he is away from the ball side and is unable to assist. X-3 is also at a disadvantage because of the distance he must cover in order to reach 0-1. Since this option is also very effective against the sinking man-to-man defense, the offensive players will have three major options from the Outside Attack with which to combat this defense.

Low Post Jumper or Pitch-off (Figures 17 and 18)

This option is started as usual by 0-1 passing the ball to 0-3 and setting up in the corner. 0-3 looks to the inside for the low post man (0-5), makes the pass to him, sets a screen to the left side of 0-5, and then sets up on the opposite low post. 0-5 now has the ball with a one-on-one situation. As he comes off 0-3's screen, he has X-5 at a disadvantage because X-5 will be unable to recover quickly enough to keep 0-5 from getting his jumper. If X-5 does recover and checks the jumper, he will be over-extended on defense, and 0-5 can drive the baseline for the jumper. X-4's defensive position on 0-4 will not allow him to help off any more than he has, and X-1 and X-2 are too far away from the ball to assist. X-3 has dropped off 0-3 to help in the basket area but also is out of position and is of little help.

Notice the defensive positions of X-4, X-5, X-3, and X-2 in Figure 18—they have maintained the defensive positions that the sinking or helping man-to-man defense strives to keep but have not covered the *Low Post Jumper or Pitch-off* option effectively. Even though this defense is designed to overcheat on the offensive big man and to protect the inside, the defensive players have lost the advantage they ordinarily would have due to the movement of the offensive players toward and away from the ball. The defense always must honor the movement of the offensive players, but on this option the movement of the offense has caused the defense to lose much of its effectiveness.

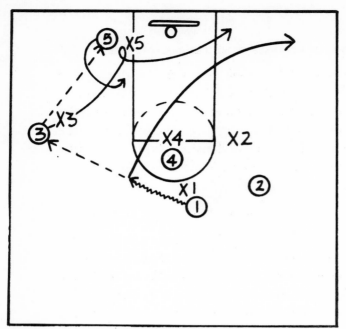

Figure 7-17
Low Post Jumper or Pitch-off
Against Sinking Man-to-Man

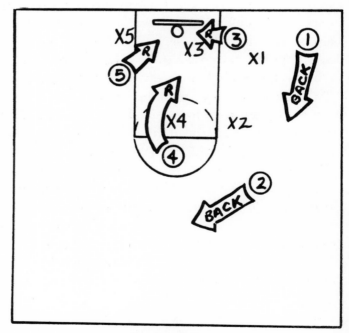

Figure 7-18
Low Post Jumper or Pitch-off
Against Sinking Man-to-Man

Two Man Through (Figures 19 and 20)

The *Two Man Through* is a follow-up to the *Low Post Jumper or Pitch-off* when 0-5, for some reason, is checked. In Figure 19, X-2 and X-4 are both playing loose, favoring the ball side and 0-5. The high post man reads 0-5's moves, realizes that 0-5 does not have the jumper, and starts his move away from the ball to screen out X-2. As soon as 0-2 sees 0-4's action, he automatically moves off the screen. 0-5 passes the ball to 0-2, who is in good position for the quick jumper or can make his move to the basket for the layup with the possibility of drawing a foul from X-3 (Figure 20). X-5 has to play the ball man (0-5) tight and cannot drop off, and X-2 is screened and cannot recover quickly enough to stop 0-2. X-1 is out of the play as far as sinking and helping are concerned, and X-4 must honor the top post man (0-4) because his move is a screening-to-the-basket move as well as a movement away from the ball. Therefore,

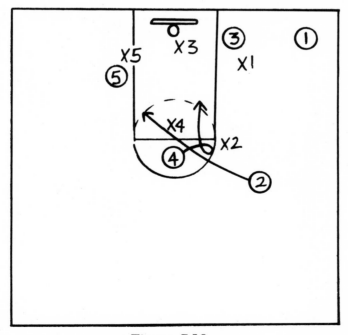

Figure 7-19
Two Man Through
Against Sinking Man-to-Man

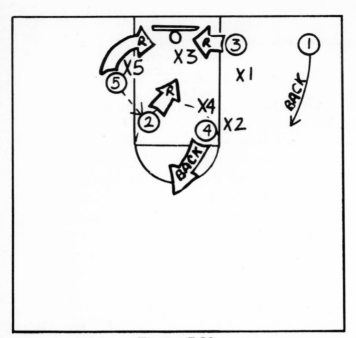

Figure 7-20
Two Man Through
Against Sinking Man-to-Man

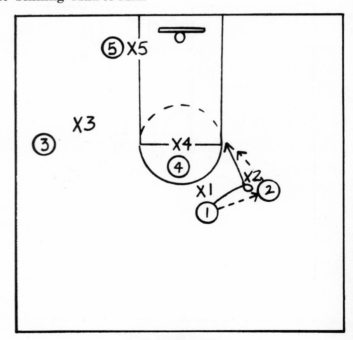

Figure 7-21
Give and Go Variation
Against Switching Man-to-Man

X-3 is the only defensive player in position to help on 0-2 if he continues to the basket for a layup.

In Figure 20 the positions of the defensive men show good floor balance on the sinking man-to-man, but again the offense has caused the defense to lose some of its effectiveness, and the defense is unable to react quickly enough to the movement of the offensive players to stop the option. This option will score many baskets for the offense during the season and will also give the outside guard the opportunity to go to the free-throw line more than he normally would.

Attacking the switching man-to-man

Some coaches dread the prospect of coming face to face with a switching man-to-man defense and may feel that a complete revision of their offensive attack will be in order. Other coaches will not go that far, but they may consider making offensive adjustments in an attempt to counteract this type of defensive attack. However, a coach whose team is thoroughly schooled in all phases of the Multiple-Continuous Offense need not fear the switching man-to-man defense. If his players have confidence in themselves and in the options, the offensive attack can be successful against this defense.

Give and Go Variation (Figure 21)

Because the defensive positions of the X-1 and X-2 defensive men in the switching man-to-man defense allow the outside guards room to maneuver, there are many possibilities on this option. Normally, X-1 will play his man about head up, and 0-1 will be veering a little to his right with his weight on his back foot. In Figure 21, X-2 is cheating a little to the left of 0-2's inside, and X-4 has dropped off 0-4 about one or two feet to allow room for X-1 and X-2 to get through screens. X-3 is playing the offensive wing man (0-3) loose, dropping off to the inside about two or three feet, but not so far that he can't get back to cover 0-3 in case he becomes the ball man or makes a move without the ball. X-5 immediately sees the one-on-one situation of both outside guards and knows that it is imperative that he honor 0-5, the low post man, because 0-5 is also in a perfect position for a one-on-one inside. This creates a tough situation for X-5 because in the switching man-to-man defense his assignment is to pick up the free shooter (either for the layup or short jumper); if he does, the low post man will be left open.

The option is started with 0-1 passing the ball to 0-2 with no interference on the part of the defense to prevent the pass. Once the movement of the offense is begun, the defensive players of the switching man-to-man will be concentrating on the switch of defensive assignments. After the pass, 0-1 makes his move to 0-2's inside foot. He then starts his reverse screen by planting his left foot to the inside foot of X-2; he stoops low and starts his reverse, holding his right arm high for a target. This results in a definite screen being set on X-2, who was waiting to pick up 0-1. The offensive guards have thus caused the defense to hang up. Although X-1 is still ready to pick up 0-2 as he comes off the screen, X-2 has been screened by 0-1 and cannot recover quickly enough on defense to pick up 0-1 before he receives the return pass from 0-2 for the quick jumper or layup.

Three Man Across (Figure 22)

This option has proved to be very successful against the switching man-to-man defense. It takes advantage of and actually forces the switch by the use of screening maneuvers by 0-3 and 0-4. In Figure 22 the situation is as follows: 0-1 has passed to 0-2 and has moved to the corner. 0-2 is set up with the ball, causing X-2 to play him honest. As soon as 0-1 gets to the corner, 0-4 begins to roll away from the ball, hesitating to screen for the wing man; X-4 will be moving with him. 0-4 moves toward the inside foot of X-3 and sets the dragging

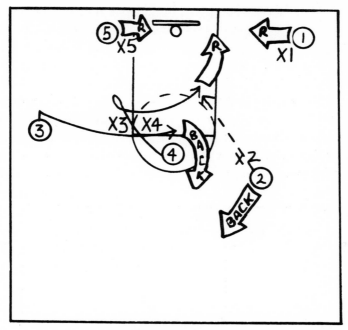

Figure 7-22
Three Man Across
Against Switching Man-to-Man

screen to the left and inside of X-3's body. As 0-4 makes his move, 0-3 fakes to the baseline and then comes over the screen tight; this is where the switch occurs. X-4 picks up 0-3, and 0-3 immediately pulls up at the free-throw line. X-3, who has moved to the screen with the wing man, is left in a difficult situation. 0-4 now has X-3 on his hip as a result of the switch, and X-3 cannot recover quickly enough to get around in front of 0-4. 0-4 knows that he has the defense beat and makes his move to the basket away from the low post man, looking for the pass. 0-2 sees that the switch has been made and hits 0-4 with the ball; 0-4 may either take the short jumper or power his way in for the layup. An alternative move if the defensive switch is not made is to run the option in its basic form—0-3 beats his man over the screen and receives the pass from 0-2 for the basket.

Low Post Jumper or Pitch-off (Figures 23 and 24)

In Figure 23 the *Low Post Jumper or Pitch-off* option is started with the outside guard passing to the wing man (0-3) and going through to set up in the corner area away from the ball. The defensive switch will be made on the wing man (0-3) and the low post man (0-5). Play is started by 0-3 passing the

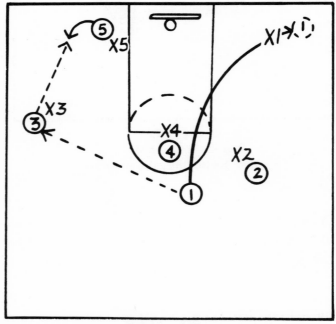

Figure 7-23
Low Post Jumper or Pitch-off
Against Switching Man-to-Man

ball to 0-5, who has pulled out to receive the pass. 0-3 then moves to the inside foot of X-5 and uses either the hesitating screen or the rolling screen on him (Figure 24). He places his right foot to X-5's outside foot and makes his reverse back to the inside. As soon as he feels pressure from X-5 and knows that the switch has been made, he makes his move to the basket. 0-3 now has X-5 on his hip and to his backside and is in good offensive position to receive a quick jump pass from 0-5. Because of the switch, X-3 is left at a disadvantage because he now has to contain 0-5, the low post man, who has a definite height advantage. 0-5 comes off the screen knowing that he may be checked by X-3, but at the same time he knows that

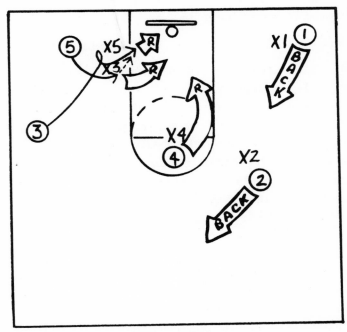

Figure 7-24
Low Post Jumper or Pitch-off
Against Switching Man-to-Man

he will be able to maneuver for position for the quick jumper or can pass back to 0-3. He is aware that this type of pass must be made swiftly and accurately in order for the option to succeed.

0-5's position with the ball is very good, as he has the ball high, ready for the jumper. If checked, he knows immediately that the quick jumper or the overhead flip pass will work. If, on the other hand, 0-5 does not get in position for the quick jumper, he can make a quick right-hand bounce pass to 0-3. The option requires good overall quickness and timing from both the wing man and the low post man. Executed properly against defensive teams that stress the switching man-to-man, the option will get some key baskets for the offensive team during the course of the game.

The Outside Reverse (Figures 25 and 26)

This option creates the situation that most coaches are always looking for and which is often referred to as the ideal situation in basketball—a big man on a little man and a little man on a big man. In Figure 25, the pattern is shown as 0-2 clears out the right side, taking X-2 with him. The positions of the other players remain the same, and the *Outside Reverse* option is now ready to be executed. In Figure 26, 0-1, who has a one-on-one situation with X-1, makes his move, dribbling the ball with his left hand to the left of 0-4's right side. He places X-1 in a poor defensive position as he reverses back over the top of 0-4's screen, and here is where the switch occurs—when X-4 picks up the outside guard (0-1). 0-1 is quick to see the switch and pulls up with the ball. 0-4 now has good offensive position on X-1, who is to his backside, so he maneuvers on the screen and picks off X-1. When 0-4 feels pressure from X-1, he moves to the basket area with a one-on-one. X-4 cannot drop off because he has ball-covering responsibility; this leaves an outside defensive guard playing the high post man. 0-1 passes the ball to 0-4, who now has good offensive position on the

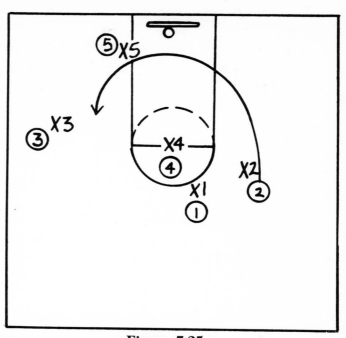

Figure 7-25
Outside Reverse
Against Switching Man-to-Man

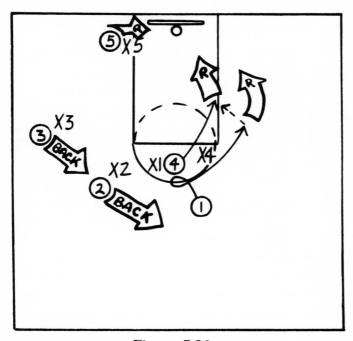

Figure 7-26
Outside Reverse
Against Switching Man-to-Man

inside for the jumper or a layup. This option can be a valuable weapon against the team that uses the switching man-to-man defense and can result in many baskets; it also tends to cause the defense to commit a number of fouls.

Summary

As your players learn and master the adjustments which may need to be made on some of the options against the different man-to-man defenses, they will gain confidence in knowing that they will be able to handle any man-to-man defense successfully with the M-C Offense. They will see that many options are impervious to common defensive techniques and that even when offensive adjustments must be made, the basic pattern remains the same. The purpose of the checklist below is to give the coach a quick rundown of the most effective options against each type of man-to-man defense with a reminder of the shooter or possible shooters on each option.

Against a Basic Man-to-Man

All the pattern options

Against a Tight (Overplaying) Man-to-Man

Basic Give and Go (0-2)
Three Man Across (0-3)
Low Post Jumper or Pitch-off (0-5)
Two Man Through (0-2)

Against a Sinking (Helping) Man-to-Man

Give and Go Variation (0-1 or 0-5)
Three Man Across (0-3)
Outside Reverse (0-1)
Low Post Jumper or Pitch-off (0-5)
Two Man Through (0-2)

Against a Switching Man-to-Man

Give and Go Variation (0-1)
Three Man Across (0-4 or 0-3)
Low Post Jumper or Pitch-off (0-5 or 0-3)
Outside Reverse (0-4)

$$8$$

M-C Offensive Strategy

Strategy always plays a major role in winning games and should be considered to be as important a phase of basketball as the fundamental drills stressed in daily practice sessions. Coaches often become so engrossed with other areas of the game, such as rebounding, pattern continuity, or free-throw percentages, that they sometimes lose sight of the role that good, sound strategy on the part of the coach can play in turning a potential loss into a victory. Because the word "strategy" can impart so many different meanings, it is often difficult to pinpoint exactly what is meant by "good strategy" in connection with basketball. It might best be summed up by saying that the coach employs good strategy when he uses every resource (plays, techniques, intensive planning) available to him at a given time that will give his team that little "extra" advantage over the opponent during a game.

Defensive strategy is every bit as important as offensive strategy. However, because this book deals with a comprehensive offensive pattern, emphasis will be placed here on offensive strategy to use in conjunction with the Multiple-Continuous

Offense. Topics discussed in this chapter include specific ways to prepare for the opponent; general game strategy, focusing on special plays; and statistics as a part of strategy.

How to prepare for a specific opponent

What areas should pregame strategy cover? In a broad sense it can include every move that the coach makes in preparation for a particular ball game—such as making certain that the players are in the best possible physical condition and are rested and ready to play on the day of the game; knowing that the team is well-schooled in its offensive pattern as well as in the defensive techniques it may use; getting the players "up" for the opponent; planning an out-of-town trip in detail, taking into consideration such factors as transportation, time of arrival, meals, and rest periods. But the foregoing listed categories are basic to coaching basketball; the good coach always attempts to cover these to the best of his ability and usually does so automatically. What, then, are the specific steps the coach can take prior to the game to satisfy himself that he is doing everything possible to help his team win that ball game? The answer to this question falls under two headings: (1) he must learn all he can about the opponent, then (2) after analyzing this information, he must formulate a game plan especially designed for use against this opponent.

What You Must Know About Your Opponent

No coach wants his team to go into a game "cold," without any previous knowledge on his part or on the part of his players of the overall size, ball-playing ability, and general offensive and defensive style of the team they will face. It is the responsibility of the coach to find out anything at all about the prospective opponent that might be of value to his ball team. This type of information can be gathered in various ways—by scouting first-hand; by watching films; by talking to other coaches whose teams have played this team earlier in the season, to name a few.

Every coach, depending on his particular brand of basketball, has his own methods of organizing his quest for information. However, certain questions about the opponent often assume top priority in the minds of many coaches, and the answers to these questions usually form the basis of their scouting report. For instance: What are the strengths of that team's outside guards—do they drive to their right more than to their left? What about their inside men—do they do most of the scoring? What type of shots are used most—jumpers? One handers? How good is their ball-handling ability? Do they pass off? How effective are their screens? What about their fakes and their peculiarities? Are they power drivers? These areas of information, along with descriptions of each individual player's strengths and weaknesses, show up in some type or form on most scouting sheets. All of this material will be invaluable in planning defensive strategy, but a good defensive attack goes only so far. Obviously you will want to stop the opponent's offensive attack if you can—that goes without saying—but a strong offensive attack on your part will have equally as much influence on the final outcome of the game. This means that you must also take a close look at the defensive strengths and weaknesses of your opponent.

One point to keep in mind when you are using the Multiple-Continuous Offense is that you can scout *positively* when analyzing your opponent's defense. You already know that you will *not* need to make any change in your basic offensive pattern as you meet various opponents but will simply need to make a few adjustments in some cases to counteract specific defensive threats. Therefore, your primary goal when scouting will not be to think negatively and make allowances for what your opponent may do on defense but to absorb their style of play in an objective manner, knowing all the while that your offensive attack, when planned strategically, *can* trip up their defense. As you watch them, run through the M-C pattern in your mind and make tentative notes as to which options might be most effective against this team. Let the following questions serve as a guide as you observe their defense:

Is their overall height the same as ours? Do they have an extra-tall post man?

Will our outside game be effective against them?

Can we run our inside game to better advantage?

What type of defense do they use as a rule?

If they use a zone, what type or types? Where is the weakness? What options will work against this zone?

What type of man-to-man defense do they use—sinking? pressure? tight? switching? What offensive options will work best against their defense?

Is their rebounding game strong? Who is their best rebounder? What will be the best way to handle him?

When you have the answers to these questions, you will be ready to begin work on your offensive game plan.

The Game Plan

The formulation of a special plan of action for each game played is probably the single most important phase of a coach's offensive (and defensive) strategy. It gives both the coach and the players a definite goal to shoot at in practice sessions prior to the game, and all effort can be expended on working on the specific options and techniques that will be most effective against the respective opponent. By using your scouting report or other data collected about this opponent, you will be in a position to analyze the strengths and weaknesses of his personnel, his defensive tactics, and his offensive pattern and can make a sound decision as to what would be the most effective method of playing him.

A comprehensive game plan should include, at the minimum, the following material:

ABOUT THE OPPONENT

Name of team

List of players' names, numbers, height and overall size, and playing position

Strengths and weaknesses of each player (on offense and on defense)

Type of defense used

Strength of inside game (weak, average, strong)

Strength of outside game (Does one guard carry the load or are both guards strong?)

Offensive and defensive shot charts from one of opponent's games

Field goal and free-throw percentages of players

YOUR GAME STRATEGY

Offensive adjustments to be made

Specific options and special plays to be used

Defensive attack to be used

As the coach carefully and thoroughly investigates all possibilities of the Multiple-Continuous Offense in determining his offensive strategy against the opponent he is to play, he will find that everything will fall right into place because of the many options and the adaptability of this type of offense. The opponent's strong points can be matched and overcome by use of the M-C attack, thus giving the coach and his players a positive advantage as they go into the game.

General game strategy

Sometimes coaches punish themselves unmercifully after their team has lost a close game by one or two points and lie awake hours on end puzzling over such questions as—Did I use the right strategy during the game? Should we have gone for the last basket with our inside option instead of our outside option? Should we have played for the foul and taken a chance on the free throw? This self-analysis is natural to a certain extent and can be considered to be one of the occupational hazards of the coaching profession. However, it can be constructive if the coach can learn from the mistakes he makes and can keep from making the same costly errors over and over again. But when a coach gets to the point where he is continually second-guessing himself, he is leaving himself wide open to criticism and will create doubt about the quality of his coaching ability both among his players and fans. When the coach learns to face a difficult situation during a ball game and can make a sound decision most of the time, he will develop confidence in himself, and this confidence will be reflected by his team.

The ability to employ strategy wisely is usually best learned from experience, but thorough preparation for critical situations that are likely to develop during a game will go a long way toward reinforcing a specific strategic decision. This part of the chapter will be concerned with positive strategy that the coach can make use of to simplify his decision-making during the crucial minutes of a game.

Use of Time-Outs

Sometimes coaches tend to be wasteful and haphazard in the use of their time-outs and call them in many instances when a word from the sideline or to a substitute that is entering the game would be sufficient. Time-outs should be used sparingly and saved for the occasion when a quick judgment or decision on the part of the coach to change defenses, attack a weakness in the opponent's defense, or make adjustments on offense is vital to the outcome of the game. There are times when other uses of the time-out are justified strategically—to bench a player who is in foul trouble and save him for use later in the game, for instance. But on the whole, you should call a time-out only when absolutely necessary. Many games have been won by the judicious use of time-outs, and many games have been lost that could have been won if the coach had had just one time-out left.

Overtime Strategy

An overtime presents a ticklish challenge to the coach, since he will have only three minutes in which to put forth a concentrated effort for the win that could not be accomplished during the game itself. Both teams will be under extra pressure because of the time limitation involved, so you have a situation that differs in many ways from the regular game. The coach must be prepared to face an overtime positively and be ready to make the quick decisions that will help his team win. Because overtime periods do not ordinarily fall under the category of the game plan, they must be considered special situations and dealt with as such.

The coach should begin by making a quick mental summary of how the game progressed during regulation time and what worked effectively for his team up to this point. Then he must make certain strategy decisions along these lines:

1. If we control the tip-off, would it be best to go on in and attempt to score? Ordinarily the answer would be "yes" because your players will be disciplined to take the shot when they gain control of the ball (see The Tip-Off Play in this chapter). Then if they do not have a good shot, they can pull up and run the overtime game strategy.

2. Are my players experienced enough to attempt to hold the ball for the full three-minute period and then try to make a last-minute score? This will depend on the effectiveness of your delay game, the strength of your last-minute play, and how well your team can hold up

under pressure in general. Keep in mind that the more a team handles the ball, the more chances it has of losing it.

3. What option would be best to run during the overtime period—one that may produce a score or one that will make the opponent foul and give us free throws? This question can pose a real problem, because it is usually impossible to predict exactly which play will work best at a given moment. You must use your judgment in relation to the options that proved most successful against this opponent during regulation time.

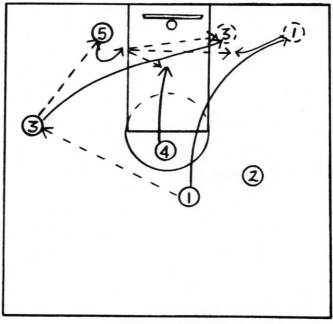

Figure 8-1
Overtime Strategy
Low Post Jumper or Pitch-off

Two examples of specific options of the M-C Offense that have proved effective in overtime situations are illustrated in Figures 1 and 2.

A. If the opposing team is using a 1-3-1 zone and is dropping back in tight, the *Low Post Jumper or Pitch-off* (Figure 1) has three advantages to offer:

    1. It requires a minimum of ball-handling—only two passes are made.
    2. 5's shooting position is close to the basket—a better gamble than an outside shot. If you force a double-team on 5 (which is likely against a 1-3-1 zone) either 3, 1, or 4 will necessarily be free to receive the pitch-off.
    3. Your players will be running an option they work on in practice and use in every game. As a result, they will be familiar with possible reactions of the defense and will also have confidence in the option itself.

B. On the other hand, if the defense is playing a type of man-to-man defense, the option from the M-C Offense that has shown its strength in this type of situation is the *Big Man—Little Man Switch* (Figure 2)—often referred to as the ideal play in basketball. Its advantages are:

    1. 1 has the option of taking the jumper if the defense does not switch.
    2. If the defense switches, 1 can penetrate closer for a layup or pass off to 4, who will be guarded by a smaller man.
    3. Again, you are using a regular option of the M-C Offense, one with which the players are already familiar. As a result, when you tell them to concentrate on this option during the overtime period,

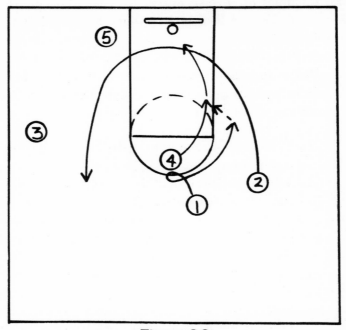

Figure 8-2
Overtime Strategy
Big Man—Little Man Switch

they will be ready to go to work with the confidence they will need to win the game.

In using the Multiple-Continuous Offense as a basic pattern,
you know that when you are faced with an overtime many of
the options from the pattern will be effective in this unexpected
situation. It relieves the coach of having to use all of his time
before the overtime begins in attempting to acquaint his
players with a certain play and expect them to go into the game
and execute it properly when they have not worked on it in
practice or used it in a game situation. The two options pre-

viously described have both been the deciding factors that helped win many overtime games. Therefore, when you use key options from this pattern, both you and your players can rest assured that the options will be dependable, since they have proved so in pressure-type situations. Properly executed, they could help win the important game that could decide a state champion.

Special Plays

Following are a group of special plays that will give your players an extra advantage in addition to the one they already have in using the Multiple-Continuous Offense. These are plays that are designed to help your team get extra baskets, to obtain an essential basket when you must have one, or to allow them to hold the ball when it is strategically necessary. If your players can execute these plays effectively, you will be that much ahead throughout the season in general, as well as when you find yourself in a tight spot. In the latter case, the special plays can make your decision-making somewhat easier. Most of these plays are not a part of the M-C pattern as such, but they have been used along with this offensive attack and have all been proved successful by teams using the M-C Offense in actual ball games.

The tip-off play

Innumerable varieties of the tip-off play are used at the beginning of games, as well as for other jump-ball situations. However, the primary concern of many teams at the tip-off is for player control of the ball, and after control is obtained, the team with the ball will go ahead and set up on offense, work its pattern, and go for the good shot or shots as planned. This is sound basketball, but at the same time the offense is not taking full advantage of controlling the tip-off. It (Team A) has given the defense (Team B) time to set up and get their rebounding strength inside. Actually, Team A has given Team

B an advantage even though it still controls the ball. In other words, Team A has lost the element of surprise.

Other advantages of having a set tip-off play that is designed to pick up the quick basket are:

1. When a team has the height advantage on jump-ball situations, the number of baskets it can make through-out the season from the tip-off play itself is impressive.
2. When both teams are about the same in the areas of height and jumping ability and your team does control the tip, you have a more than even chance of scoring a quick basket.
3. When Team A gets the ball and goes with it, Team B will tend to become as conscious of getting back on defense as it is of trying to control the tip.

The following tip-off play is one that has been proved effec-tive and can be used in each game you play, both at the begin-ning of the game and after half-time. Many opponents, after scouting you, feel that they can handle it, but because of its variations it will still pick up a number of baskets for you throughout the season.

PROCEDURE

If you have a slight height advantage, the defense will set up in the manner shown in Figure 3. 0-1 and 0-2 are lined up straddling the half-court line. As soon as the ball is tossed up by the official they will flare out toward their respective out-of-bounds lines and then move on into the basket at wide angles. The play is started by 0-5 tipping the ball to 0-4.

> VARIATION A (Figure 3): As soon as 0-4 controls, he pivots with the ball in close to his belt buckle and then passes to 0-1 or 0-2, who will drive on in for the layup. As soon as the pass is made, 0-4 continues to the basket, looking for a possible return pass, or is in perfect position to rebound if the shot is missed.

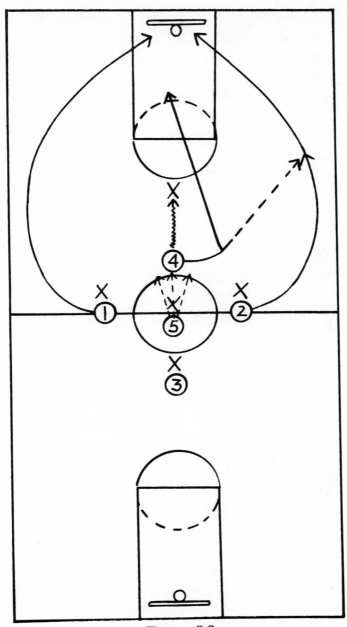

Figure 8-3
Special Plays
Tip-off Play (Variation A)

VARIATION *B* (Figure 4): 0-4, after controlling the ball, can drive right or left toward the basket with the ball and force the defensive man to stop him. When the defensive man comes to him, 0-4 now can pass to 0-1 or 0-2, who will go in for the layup.

VARIATION *C* (Figure 5): 0-4 turns, and makes the pass to 0-2, who is free on the side. 0-2 goes on in with the ball and forces the defensive man to take him. He then makes a bounce or jumper pass to 0-1, who is in good position for a layup. 0-4 moves to the basket to rebound. This option can be worked to either side, depending on the best outlet pass for 0-4 to use.

Some opponents, when they see how you work this play and feel that you will control the tip, will give you the tip and drop off in an attempt to stop the fast-break move to the basket. Many teams will double-team your 0-4 man, but in order to still maintain an advantage, have your 0-5 center make a fist with his right hand or left hand as an indicator to 0-4 as to which direction the ball will be tipped. He will not want to tip it to 0-4's extreme right or left but can vary it just enough so that 0-4 will be able to adjust and still get the ball. The fist signal should be subtle, not an extended-arm type; 0-4 simply needs to look at 0-5's hands before the jump to get the signal. The straight-ahead tip is executed with no hand signal at all.

The out-of-bounds play

Coaches run across all types of out-of-bounds plays during the course of a season. Many of these plays will be fundamental, while others require some thinking on the part of the offensive players. They will vary in nature from the spur-of-the-moment free-lance play to the complex play designed for strategic purposes. Some coaches may use six or more different types of out-of-bounds plays during the regular season while others manage with only one or maybe two. Many out-of-bounds plays are

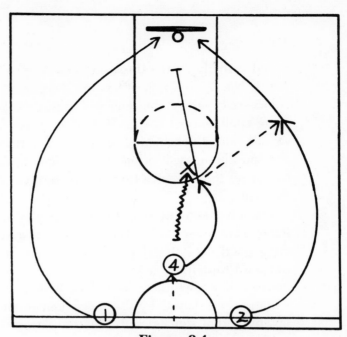

Figure 8-4
Special Plays
Tip-off Play (Variation B)

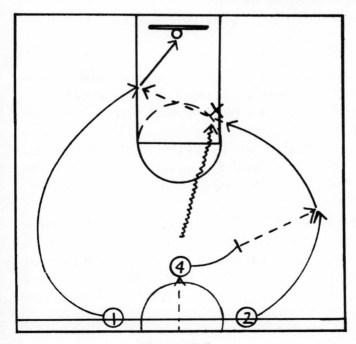

Figure 8-5
Special Plays
Tip-off Play (Variation C)

keyed verbally by the throw-in man, who calls out the play as No. 1, No. 2, or No. 3; others are designated by the names of colors—red, blue, green; and still others are keyed by number-letter combinations such as 1-A, 2-A, or 3-A. The use of verbal signals can be detrimental because the defense, through scouting and filming, will often pick up these keys and either get a basket on the offensive throw-in themselves or gain control of the ball.

The advantages of an out-of-bounds play such as the following one are many. (1) It is designed as a scoring play and provides good floor shooting position; (2) it is simple in nature but hard to defense; (3) extra pressure is put on the defense because it knows that the offense will try to score; (4) its variations are keyed by the movement of the high post man, not by verbal signals; and (5) the players know that it will work and will have confidence in it. Many teams use the basic setup indicated in this play, but with different offensive movement. The moves outlined here have been proved to be extremely advantageous in scoring key baskets.

PROCEDURE

In Figure 6, the positions of both the offensive and defensive players are shown as the play begins. You can see the advantage of having the defense in a box-type setup, especially from the standpoint of the offense in setting screens. Three basic moves can be made from this setup by 0-4 that will key the variation of the play that is to be used. The moves of the other offensive players will depend on this key.

VARIATION A (Figure 7): 0-4 moves to the corner, taking X-4 with him. X-4 is prone to honor 0-4 because he is to the ball side; if he stays and helps on the inside, 0-4 can easily receive the ball and be the shooter. Thus X-4 normally will go with 0-4 because of his defensive responsibility.

0-5, the low man away from the ball, moves to set a screen on X-2 and then rolls to the basket. If the defense switches here, 0-5 will be open on the screen; if they do not switch, 0-2 should be free. 0-3 will drop back to the top of the key for defensive responsibility as well as for floor balance. The pass from the throw-in man, 0-1, can now be made either to 0-2 or 0-5 for the basket.

VARIATION B (Figure 8): The play is begun by 0-4's move to set a screen on 0-5's defensive man; after his screen is set, 0-4 then rolls back to the ball. 0-5 comes off 0-4's screen

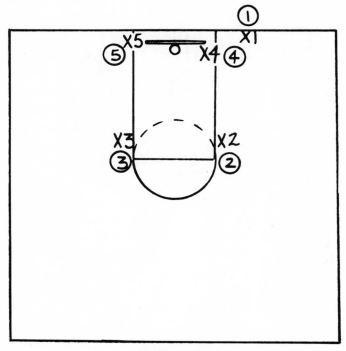

Figure 8-6
Special Plays
Out-of-Bounds Play (Basic Setup)

looking for the pass. Again there is the possibility of a switch in defensive players. If it is made, 0-4 will be the shooter; if the defense plays honest, then 0-5 will be the shooter. 0-2 and 0-3 will move to the area of the free-throw line extended for balance. The defense must move with them as they also are in good shooting position. The throw-in man can now make his pass to 0-4 or 0-5 for the basket.

VARIATION C (Figure 9): Here you have the two-on-two situation with 0-4 and 0-2 and their defensive men. 0-4

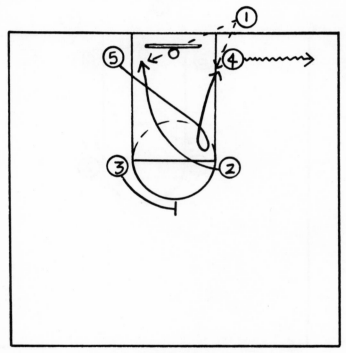

Figure 8-7
Special Plays
Out-of-Bounds Play (Variation A)

moves and sets a rolling screen on 0-2's defensive man. 0-2 fakes to go to his left, but instead comes back to the right on the screen set by 0-4. Here again the defense may switch; if so, 0-4 will have the advantage, and 0-1 will pass the ball to him. If the defense does not switch, 0-2 will have the advantage and will receive the pass from 0-1. 0-5 has cleared away from the ball to allow plenty of room for the maneuver, and 0-3 will drop back to the top of the key for defense as well as floor balance. 0-2's possibility of going to the side he fakes to can be used if X-2 is fighting

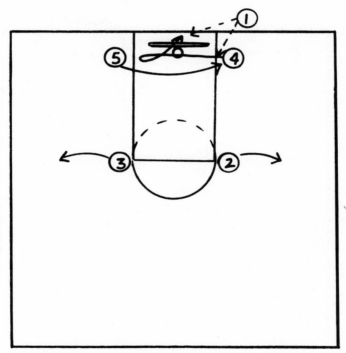

Figure 8-8
Special Plays
Out-of-Bounds Play (Variation B)

or overplaying the screen set by 0-4. The two-on-two situation here is ideal and, properly utilized, can be very profitable for the offense.

There should be a definite place in every coach's game plan for the out-of-bounds play. When running a play such as the one previously described, your first objective is to score; however, you will still have definite ball control if you fail to shoot. If the opportunity to score presents itself, then your players should shoot the ball; if not, then they will be ready to set up

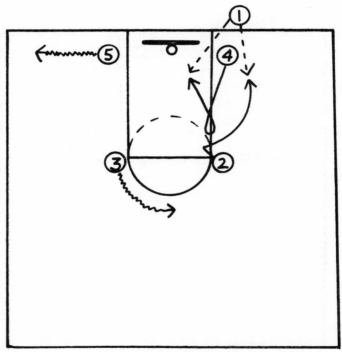

Figure 8-9
Special Plays
Out-of-Bounds Play (Variation C)

and work some option of the pattern. The consistent success of any out-of-bounds play always depends on the amount of time spent on it in practice as well as the confidence the players have in executing the play. Many times the game is tied going into the end of the first half, and the ball is given out-of-bounds to a team with three seconds left on the clock. If you have a sound out-of-bounds play, then you can go to the dressing room two points ahead; this will often give your players a psychological boost that will help motivate their second-half performance.

The last-minute play

When a team finds itself in an end-of-the-game situation where one crucial basket means the difference between winning or losing, it will be to its advantage to be able to run a play that (1) has proved to be a "point-getter"; (2) provides good shooting position near the basket; (3) has the best rebounders in close to put the ball up again if the first shot is missed; and (4) is a move with which the players are completely familiar and which they can execute with confidence.

Two options of the Multiple-Continuous Offense fit every requirement outlined here for the effective last-minute play—the *Three Man Around* (Figure 10) and the *Two Man Through* (Figure 11). Both of these options have proved successful in "clutch" situations, and because they are a part of the pattern, your players should be able to run either one with assurance. In each option the shooter will be close enough to the basket for a short jumper or, in some cases, can penetrate in for a lay-up. Too, both of your post men will be in good rebounding position, as will be at least one additional player. An added advantage of these two options lies in the fact that both of them tend to cause the defense to foul; this might get the free throw that you need to put you ahead in the last few seconds of the game.

Obviously, use of last-minute plays is not limited to end-of-

the-game situations. They also can be of benefit in the case
where your team gets possession of the ball with about a minute
to go before the end of the quarter or the half, and you want
the players (for any number of strategic reasons) to hold out
for the "one shot." Both the *Three Man Around* and the *Two
Man Through* will be effective in any last-minute situation;
but, as with the other options of the pattern, their ultimate
success will depend on proper execution, which can only be
accomplished by concentrated drill during your daily practice
sessions.

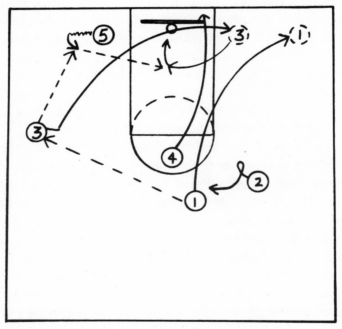

Figure 8-10
Special Plays
Last-Minute Plays (Three Man Around)

The delay game

The main purpose of any type of delay game is to allow the offense to maintain sustained control of the ball during certain crucial minutes of a ball game. Although this technique can be employed at any time during the course of the game, most coaches will use it primarily at the end when there are only two or three minutes remaining on the clock. Often, teams will use their basic patterns for their delay game; others will run from an entirely different setup when they want to hold the

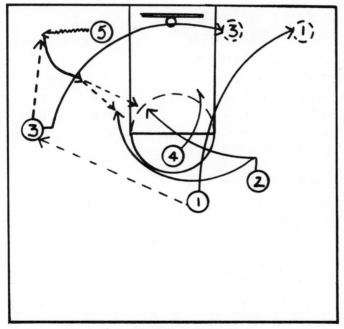

Figure 8-11
Special Plays
Last-Minute Plays (Two Man Through)

ball. Regardless of the type of delay game you use, plan to concentrate on perfecting it in practice sessions so that your players will have confidence in it and will be able to run it smoothly and effectively whenever the situation warrants its use. Knowing that you have a sound delay game will simplify your decision-making and you will be better able to handle such problems as: Should we hold the ball and not shoot until five seconds are left on the clock? Should we shoot when we have a good shot regardless of how much time is left? Can we hit the free throws under pressure if fouled? These situations, along with others, have to be worked out and can be with the proper delay game. The opponent who knows that you have an effective delay game will have more respect for your team and as a result may try to vary his defensive attack (to your advantage) against your delay game.

The type of delay game that has proved most successful for teams using the Multiple-Continuous Offense is labeled "40 or 41 Delay Game." The last numeral provides the key as to which delay game the players are to run. Used properly, this type of delay game will be a definite asset to the coach and to his team.

40 Delay Game

This type of delay game is used in the situation where the offensive team is ahead by six or eight points with two or three minutes left on the clock, and the coach feels that he can maintain that advantage by holding the ball. The 40 Delay Game is run from the regular M-C pattern, and no attempt is made at the basket. Since the defense will spread out when it recognizes the stall, the offense will have plenty of room in which to operate and can run the regular options over and over without taking a shot.

41 Delay Game

In the 41 Delay Game, the "1" indicates to the players that they can take the good shot (the layup is emphasized here) when it presents itself. If a player has to work for the basket at all, then he foregoes the shot and continues the stall until a good shot becomes available. When running the 41 Delay Game, the players will not use the basic offensive pattern but will set up as indicated in Figure 12. The advantages of using this type of setup are (1) the defense must spread out; (2) the one-on-one situation exists; and (3) the basket area is open. Many coaches use this basic setup for their delay game but teach no specific moves to go along with it. The free-lance continuous movement described in the following paragraph will make your delay game twice as effective.

Procedure

In Figure 12, 0-1 starts the movement; he passes the ball to 0-2 and then moves to 0-4's original position. 0-4, in the meantime, has rotated, filling the spot vacated by 0-1. 0-3 comes up to meet the pass from 0-2 (Figure 13), and after receiving the ball moves to 0-2's position. On 0-3's move 0-1 immediately moves to 0-3's corner; and 0-2, after he has made the pass to 0-3, moves to the spot vacated by 0-1. Emphasis is placed on (1) the passer's movement away from the ball after his pass and (2) the importance of the offside players moving as necessary to keep the defense spread out as well as remaining aware of the possibility of a return pass being made. 0-5's responsibility at the high post position is to stay alert and be ready to help out by receiving the ball whenever a teammate is double-teamed by the defense. He then passes off to the player who is open, and the movement continues. Any time a player sees an opportunity for a layup, he takes it, but only if he can do so without pressure from the defense.

In the 41 Delay Game the offensive players are able to maintain balanced floor position at all times. They do not have to "freeze" with the ball because they know what movements are likely to be made by their teammates and, therefore, will lose the ball fewer times during this crucial period when control of the ball is essential. You will find that the offense will be awarded numerous free throws as a result of their continual movement, and the importance of making the "one and one" under these circumstances cannot be overemphasized by the coach. This delay game can give the offensive team a tremendous psychological boost; the reward is player confidence whenever they are faced with this type of situation.

Delay Game Practice Drill: Game of Ten

As the 40 and 41 Delay Games are stressed in practice sessions, a competitive game can be made with them. This type

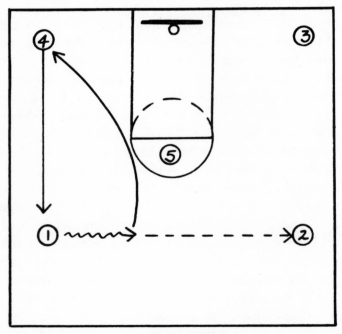

Figure 8-12
Special Plays
41 Delay Game

of competitive drill allows the players to gain experience similar to what they will have in a game under the same conditions. The use of the clock adds to the game-like situation and stimulates the players to put forth every effort to come out on top. The drill can be used with either of the two delay games.

PROCEDURE

Ten points constitutes game. The game is started with a jump ball, and the team that controls (Team A) sets up on offense. If it controls the ball for 10 seconds, one point is scored; Team A then takes the ball out-of-bounds. If it can hold the ball for

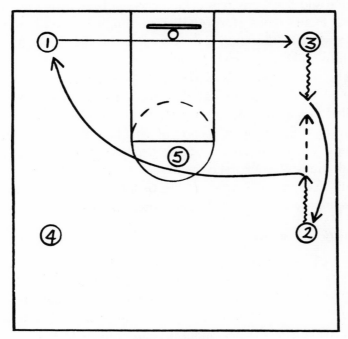

Figure 8-13
Special Plays
41 Delay Game

10 seconds after the throw-in, another point is added to its score—a total of two points for Team A. If, on the next throw-in, Team B (the defense) steals the ball, it receives one point and the ball out-of-bounds. This makes an overall score of 3. If Team B can control the ball for 10 full seconds, it receives another point; the total score is now 4—Team A has 2 points and Team B has 2 points. The drill continues until the score reaches 10 points (the final score might end up 8-2, 6-4, or perhaps 5-5). If the score is tied at the end of the game, a jump ball is called, and the team that controls has the last 10 seconds to win. No actual field goals are attempted during this game, but if a foul is committed, the player who is fouled is awarded a "one and one"; any points he makes on free throws are added to his team's score. If a free-throw attempt is missed, no points are awarded; the team that rebounds the ball takes it out-of-bounds and the game continues.

The competitiveness of the drill gives the players an incentive to work hard, and as they work they will become more skilled in maintaining control of the ball under pressure. Have your manager keep a record of ball-handling mistakes, bad passes, and the number of times a player gets trapped so that weak areas of your delay game can be assessed and strengthened. The carryover value of this drill to actual game situations is as important as any drill that is used in other areas.

Statistics as a part of strategy

Statistics can play a very important role as the coach plans his strategy because they serve as a measuring stick for his own players as well as for the opponents he will play. By using statistics, the coach is able to put his finger immediately on the effectiveness of the personnel in many phases of the game and can pinpoint weak areas. Coaches compile statistics on the opponents in order to gauge their overall team strength in the areas of rebounding, ball-handling capabilities, and shooting ability, as well as to analyze the strong and weak points of each team member. At the same time, it is most important to keep records of your own squad so that you will be able to keep abreast of the progress your players make as the season progresses.

Current team statistics can immediately give you the answer to the following questions: Is our scoring balanced or do one or two players tend to take all the shots? Who has the best field goal percentage from the Outside Attack of the M-C Offense? From the Inside Attack? Who has the highest free-throw percentage? Who is the best rebounder? The best assist player? The best defensive player? Who makes the most violations? Who leads in number of lost balls? Who makes the most bad passes? The coach uses these areas and others in determining who his starters will be, and he will also have a ready answer if questioned as to the reason one player is playing ahead of another. Too, when using the M-C Offense in particular, statistics give you a firm basis for making player assignments, allowing you better to place each man in his proper position.

Players normally get better and stronger with experience and maturity during the season. Weekly progress reports can be made up for each player until the season begins and from then on after every five games. At the end of the year, you can give the players a recap of their totals in each phase of the game. Also, team statistics can be posted on the bulletin board, giving the players a chance to compare their performances; this will definitely motivate them to strive for improvement in the areas where they are weak. Poster-board bar graphs can be kept up to date and will also act as a motivating force to the players. Areas such as the following can be charted:

> Free throws attempted, made, percentage.
> Field goals attempted, made, percentage.
> Number of offensive, defensive, and total rebounds; rebound average per game.

Number of bad passes, violations, total lost balls.
Number of assists.
Team totals on all of the foregoing.

Well-kept statistics will give the coach an extra tool with which to assess his team members individually and as a whole and will allow the coach the opportunity of getting the maximum from his players. No matter what type of offense or defense is used, statistics play a vital role and can make the difference between a winning ball club and a losing one.

9

Conclusion: Using the M-C Offensive to Full Potential

After having read this book you should be convinced of the potential of the Multiple-Continuous Offense. You have become familiar with its many advantages and the manner in which it can be utilized most effectively. You have seen that the pattern is adaptable and can be used in the average situation found in most high schools as it emphasizes teamwork, player cooperation, and use of the skills of all five men on the court instead of requiring specialized talents or unusually tall personnel. The M-C Offense has proved itself to be an offensive attack that can produce a winning basketball team. However, as with any other offense, success will not come automatically. Many factors will have a part in determining how effective it will be—the attitude of the players themselves, the amount of time spent on it in practice sessions, as well as such items as the proficiency of your defensive attack and the quality of your program as a whole.

Probably the most important factor is your attitude as a coach. You must have a thorough knowledge of the M-C Offense and be convinced that it can help your team be a winner. Before you even think about introducing the offense to your players you must be certain that you are well-grounded in its basic principles. Following is a checklist of the phases in which you should be well-versed:

Pattern Positions

Go over each position separately; go over each move; know each position's playing area; know the role of each player in the pattern (Chapter 2, especially diagrams 1 through 5).

Drills

Know the purpose of each specialized drill and how it will relate to the pattern (Chapter 3).

Basic Options

Study the basic options; become thoroughly familiar with each one; be sure you know: (a) the responsibilities of each player on each option, (b) which players can shoot from each option, (c) which players will rebound on each option, and (d) the underlying continuity of the pattern (Chapters 4 and 5).

Ways to Combat Defensive Tactics

Know automatically which options to use against various defensive situations (Chapters 6 and 7).

Offensive Strategy

Be familiar with the basic strategy to be used with this attack. Be able to improvise and combine options to fit every situation you might face. Plan a series of special plays and consider them as a part of your attack (Chapter 8).

When you are ready to teach the Multiple-Continuous Offense to your players, know the offense so well and present it in such a way that your enthusiasm about it will be reflected by them. Let them know that you definitely feel that this offense will help them win games. Be positive! Make certain that every player knows his role in the pattern and has a thorough knowledge of his moves on each option. And finally, remember that although your players should have a basic concept of the pattern as a whole, *you* are the one who must be aware of all the "ins and outs" of this offense because *you* will make the strategic decisions. *You* will be the mastermind of the attack.

Index

A

Abilities of players, evaluation of, 29-31

Adjustments to counteract various defensive tactics, 34-39

Advantages of M-C offense, 15-22
definition of, 15-16
frustration of opponent, 19-20
1-3-1 offense, comparison with basic, 16-18
other, 20-22
shuffle, comparison with, 18-19

Advantages of specialized drills, 42-43

Attitude of player, evaluation of, 30

Average personnel, multiple-continuous offense designed for, 20-21

B

Back Door against 1-2-2 zone defense, 123-125

Back door or pitch-out in inside attack, 98-100

Ball-handling skills in players, evaluation of, 31

Basic drills for M-C offense, 62-67
board tip, 64-66
competitive rebounding, 66-67
star pep, 63-64
star shooting, 64

Basic man-to-man defense, attacking, 135-136

Big man-little man switch in outside attack, 85-89
overtime situation, advantages in, 175-176

Board tip drill, 64-66

Box-and-1 zone, attacking, with M-C offense, 130-132

C

Checklist for coach of essentials of M-C offense, 198

Competitive rebounding drill, 66-67

Confusion of opponent by use of multiple-continuous offense, 19-20

Consistency of pattern movement, analysis of, 24

Creating big man-little man switch, 85-87

D

Defenses, effectiveness of multiple-continuous offense against all, 22

Defensive big man, reduction of threat by multiple-continuous offense, 21-22

Delay game, 189-194
"40 or 41 delay game," 190-192
practice drill, 192-194

Drills for M-C offense, 41-67
basic, 62-67
board tip, 64-66
competitive rebounding, 66-67
star pep, 63-64
star shooting, 64
specialized, 42-62
advantages, 42-43
nine, 43-62
purpose, 42

F

Fake and step-back method, 146

Familiarization of players with all moves by use of pattern-oriented drills, 43

Figure Eight drill, 62

Five Up against:
1-2-2 zone defense, 121-123
against 1-3-1 zone, 109-112